MW00333206

About Island Press

Since 1984, the nonprofit organization Island Press has been stimulating, shaping, and communicating ideas that are essential for solving environmental problems worldwide. With more than 800 titles in print and some 40 new releases each year, we are the nation's leading publisher on environmental issues. We identify innovative thinkers and emerging trends in the environmental field. We work with world-renowned experts and authors to develop cross-disciplinary solutions to environmental challenges.

Island Press designs and executes educational campaigns in conjunction with our authors to communicate their critical messages in print, in person, and online using the latest technologies, innovative programs, and the media. Our goal is to reach targeted audiences—scientists, policymakers, environmental advocates, urban planners, the media, and concerned citizens—with information that can be used to create the framework for long-term ecological health and human well-being.

Island Press gratefully acknowledges major support of our work by The Agua Fund, The Andrew W. Mellon Foundation, Betsy & Jesse Fink Foundation, The Bobolink Foundation, The Curtis and Edith Munson Foundation, Forrest C. and Frances H. Lattner Foundation, G.O. Forward Fund of the Saint Paul Foundation, Gordon and Betty Moore Foundation, The JPB Foundation, The Kresge Foundation, The Margaret A. Cargill Foundation, New Mexico Water Initiative, a project of Hanuman Foundation, The Overbrook Foundation, The S.D. Bechtel, Jr. Foundation, The Summit Charitable Foundation, Inc., V. Kann Rasmussen Foundation, The Wallace Alexander Gerbode Foundation, and other generous supporters.

The opinions expressed in this book are those of the author(s) and do not necessarily reflect the views of our supporters.

THE FUTURE OF THE SUBURBAN CITY

The Future of the Suburban City

Lessons from Sustaining Phoenix

Grady Gammage Jr.

Washington | Covelo | London

Island Press is a trademark of The Center for Resource Economics.

Keywords: Air conditioning, air quality, annexation, climate change, global
warming, haboob, Hohokam, light rail, residential density, single-family home,
suburban city, suburban sprawl, sustainability, shopping center, solar energy,
Sun Corridor, Sunbelt cities, urban heat island, urban resilience, transportation,
water management

Library of Congress Control Number: 2015953755

Printed on recycled, acid-free paper ✪

Manufactured in the United States of America
10 9 8 7 6 5 4 3 2

Contents

	Prologue: Getting through the Haboob	*ix*
	Acknowledgments	*xiii*
Chapter 1.	Suburbs, Sprawl, and Sustainability	1
Chapter 2.	Just Add Water	23
Chapter 3.	Coping with Heat	55
Chapter 4.	Transportation and the Suburban City	75
Chapter 5.	Houses, Shopping Centers, and the Fabric of Suburbia	93
Chapter 6.	Jobs and the Economy of Cities in the Sand	125
Chapter 7.	Politics, Resilience, and Survival	153
	Afterword: Planning to Stay	*167*
	Notes	*171*
	Index	*185*

Prologue: Getting through the Haboob

Ahwatukee is a suburb of a suburban city. Nestled against the back side of South Mountain, it is now part of the City of Phoenix, annexed in the late 1970s after a skirmish with Tempe. It was developed as a low-amenity, early-generation master-planned community. Ten miles from Tempe and fifteen from downtown Phoenix, it seemed "far out" when it was first built and so was initially marketed to retirees. The first houses that were built there are deed-restricted to people over 50 and were initially priced "from the $50s."

Today, Ahwatukee is a quintessential slice of suburban America. It has a broad variety of single-family homes, not very many jobs, an increasing number of apartments, a few decent restaurants, and a bunch of empty big-box stores. The schools are decent but underfunded, and the parks are crowded with sports teams but few trees. Ahwatukee is where I live.

My wife, Karen, and I built a custom house there in the 1980s and raised our kids; now we're empty nesters. My swimming pool doesn't get much use, but filling it in would disrupt the aesthetic of the backyard. I struggle to keep a small patch of grass green. The trend is to put in artificial turf, but it's shockingly expensive and still looks tacky, even when it includes fake "thatch." I haven't installed solar panels yet; they would look out of place sticking above the parapets on my low, Santa Fe–style house.

My backyard looks south of the City toward the Gila River Indian Community and the farmlands of Pinal County. We can see the monsoon storms that swell up from the south in the summertime. On this particular evening, Karen and I stood out there, hoping for rain. The temperature was still about 106 degrees. A massive wall of dust was coming up from the south, thousands of feet high. It looked like the wrath of God.

When I was a kid, we called them "dust storms," and we would put on swim masks to go outside and run around when the dust was thickest. Now the TV weather people delight in the term *haboob*, partly because it's fun to say and partly, I suspect, because it sounds vaguely terrorist-inspired. "Team coverage" from all the local stations will deploy to film the haboob with their hyperbolic style, suggesting that the apocalypse is nigh.

To live in a city named after a bird that periodically immolates itself is to invite scrutiny. "Phoenix" is self-evidently a brand of improbability, fragility, impermanence. The city sits marooned in the desert, impossibly dry, dangerously hot, and presumptively unsustainable. It was named Phoenix because it sits atop the ruins of the Hohokam civilization that represented a several-hundred-year-long adaptation to desert life based on growing crops with water from the Salt River. At their height, the Hohokam settlements included dense urban villages, sports venues, and even multi-story "condos" like Casa Grande. Their civilization sounds eerily familiar.

For generations, modern Arizonans wondered what happened to the Hohokam and why their archeological records vanished sometime around 1450. In 2008, a team of scholars concluded that the population decline wasn't nearly as sudden as had previously been thought. Rather, over a period of about 150 years the population shrank as the result of a long-term drought, stressing crop yields and increasing social tension. High-density nodes formed around the best-irrigated areas. In between those nodes, canal maintenance began to suffer. People started leaving, and those who were left assimilated into smaller, lower-density and less distinctive cultures.

At their height, the Hohokam population was about 40,000. Metro Phoenix today is just over 4 million. As I watched the haboob approach, it was hard not to think about the Hohokam. With the

Figure 0.1. Pueblo Grande was the original Hohokam settlement on the bank of the Salt River. It is now a City of Phoenix park, located next to the airport. (Source: Pueblo Grande Museum, City of Phoenix)

dust getting closer, I headed back inside to my filtered, sealed, and air-conditioned home. The sky grew darker, the dust descended, and we watched it roll through.

The haboob lasted about forty-five minutes, and the biggest consequence was that my pool got really, really dirty.

Acknowledgments

This book grew out of a conversation with Rob Melnick from the Global Institute of Sustainability (GIOS) at Arizona State University (ASU). I told Rob that I was thinking of redoing *Phoenix in Perspective*, which I had written in the late 1990s, and he suggested that I focus on the broader question of the sustainability of places like Phoenix. Our colleague Ann Kinzig introduced me to Island Press as a potential publisher. GIOS provided financial support for a major chunk of my time to work on this project and also gave me a terrific graduate research assistant, Van Patterson, during the spring of 2015. Van pulled together a host of efforts to rate, rank, and quantify sustainability, set up a series of interviews, and was a great sounding board. At Island Press, Heather Boyer was a perfect editor—constructive, quick, and engaging.

The Morrison Institute for Public Policy at ASU was generous in understanding my limited ability to work on other projects there while this one was under way. Dan Hunting, Sapna Gupta, Andrea Whitsett, Sarah Porter, and all of the staff there were helpful in finding information on a wide variety of subjects. Many of the Morrison Institute reports from the past decade found their way into the book.

The attorneys and staff at Gammage and Burnham were generous in understanding my reduction in billable hours while this work was under way. My legal assistant, Terri McEuen, did all of the typing and a fair amount of fact-checking, and she was of invaluable assistance throughout the process.

Finally, I must thank my wife, Karen, for her patience as I hyperventilated about this project and for her unending capacity to hold my life together.

Chapter 1

Suburbs, Sprawl, and Sustainability

Cities are living organisms. They grow, flourish, wither, and sometimes die. Throughout history, once-robust cities have reached points of economic obsolescence and have declined. Some vanish altogether, like Babylon and Ur. Others, like Venice, become essentially museums of themselves. Some survive, but shrink dramatically—like Detroit or St. Louis.

St. Louis, "the Gateway to the West," was once the greatest boomtown in America. Situated on the Mississippi, St. Louis saw the river as the forever-paramount avenue of commerce in the United States. But it turned out that railroads were more important than the river, and Chicago placed its bet on railroads. In the 1890s, St. Louis was the fourth-largest city in America. In 2014, it was the sixtieth-largest city in America, with about 318,000 people. Today, Mesa, Arizona, has nearly 150,000 more people than St. Louis.[1]

1

Figure 1.1. Aerial view of the Ahwatukee Foothills area of Phoenix. (© Shutterstock: Tim Roberts Photography)

As the world becomes ever more urban, the long-term prospects for the survival of individual cities is often critiqued, ranked, and debated. The term *sustainability* is the most frequent rubric of conversation. The new cities of postwar America generally fare poorly in these discussions. Built around the automobile and the single-family home, these cities are casually indicted for profligate resource consumption, low-density sprawl, and a mindless addiction to real estate development.

Even before Andrew Ross labeled Phoenix "the world's least sustainable place" in his 2011 book *Bird on Fire*, the city often served as an exemplar of such a place: isolated, dry, hot, and surely one of the most improbable and therefore least sustainable big cities on earth.[2] Bill deBuys wrote about the city's impending doom from climate change: "If cities were stocks, you'd short Phoenix."[3]

Despite the criticism of the "suburban cities" that arose in the last half of twentieth century America, Las Vegas, Phoenix, Salt Lake City, Dallas, Tucson, San Bernardino, and San Diego continue to be among the fastest growing places in the United States. In December 2014, the *Economist* looked at world cities.[4] In a discussion of the planet's future, the "great urbanisation" (as they spell it) is frequently invoked: a world in which most people live in cities. The point of their analysis is that these global cities are looking increasingly suburban. Chinese, Indian, and Brazilian cities are all experiencing declines in density. Since 1970, Beijing's density has dropped by 75 percent. (Even at that, it is still about five times more dense than places like Phoenix.) Worldwide, the few cities that are becoming more dense are places like Los Angeles, Las Vegas, and Phoenix, which started out with very low density to begin with.

More than sixty years ago, the late Jane Jacobs examined the plight of American cities in one of the most insightful pieces of urban analysis ever written, *The Death and Life of Great American Cities*.[5] The book is remembered as a screed against the perils of city planning, which she saw as an interference with the natural evolution of cities and the complex and intricate relationships among individual land uses. Today, her book tends to be remembered as a paean to places like Greenwich Village: pedestrian environments with a rich mix of uses; a layered texture of building types, sizes, and ages; and an ongoing generational drama played out in a largely unplanned "ballet of the street." Jacobs would not have liked places like Phoenix. Cities that grew in the latter half of the twentieth century were based not on intricate pedestrian interactions but on the convenience of automobiles. But perhaps Jacobs's greatest gift to thinking about the nature of cities was her application of observational logic to thinking about the way cities evolve, grow, and possibly die. She taught us that cities are the products of millions of individual decisions about how people want to live, to work, to recreate, and to interact. Those individual, incremental decisions are made in a particular context: an economic context as the city grows and matures; a technological context that exists for horizontal or vertical movement at different speeds and varying distances. Cities also evolve in a political context—a determination of how to negotiate the social contract between the needs of society and the rights of the individual.

Jacobs's observational insights were applied to the great industrial cities of America. Such cities were the products of the Industrial Revolution, the invention of the elevator, the streetcar, and the subway, and the employment of millions of workers in high-density production industries. She saw the problems created when those kinds of cities were subject suddenly to countervailing forces like the automobile, the airplane, and a political desire for more centralized planning.

It is possible to apply Jacobs's analytical tools to the cities that grew up later than did her favorite places. The same forces that operated to cause decline in the great cities of the nineteenth and early twentieth centuries were also operating to shape the cities of the latter half of the twentieth century. These changing forces dispersed populations that had previously been concentrated. The first, most obvious, and most examined of these urban change agents was the automobile, which made it possible for any given piece of property to be easily accessible with just a dirt road. The automobile served as an agent of destruction to the older industrial cities that had been built around streetcar commuting or pedestrian activity. Cars dispersed cities, causing a decline in the overall population density of older places. The automobile also begat the parking lot, an urban dead zone—hostile to pedestrians, hot, and uninviting.

City populations were also being dispersed by the growing dominance of the single-family detached home as a preferred lifestyle. The individual detached home had long been an aspirational goal of Americans, of course, but as the twentieth century rolled on it became attainable for ever-larger numbers. Together, the automobile and the single-family home would rewrite the nature of American urbanization.

While these forces were operating to disperse the American population, there were simultaneously countervailing forces in operation.[6] The first of these was the rise of air travel as a dominant mode of interurban transportation. When the railroad became the means to getting from one place to another, small- and medium-sized cities were well served by tracks running through town with stops for goods and passengers. Air travel, on the other hand, is a force of concentration. Airports take a lot of room and cannot be too close together. The benefit of travel by air is speed, and landing too often results in slowing down that advantage.

As the American West began to urbanize, the region faced particular challenges that also played out in forces of concentration. The greatest of these challenges was the need to capture, store, and deliver water to particular locations. "Beyond the hundredth meridian," in Wallace Stegner's memorable phrase,[7] where there is less than ten inches of rain per year, water provides an organizing principle, a dominating urban force, a power of concentrating population where water delivery makes a city possible.

These forces of concentration and dispersal, coupled with the advent of zoning and planning played out in the context of postwar American growth, resulted in a different urban fabric. These forces created the suburban city. The *Economist's* review noted that suburbanization has been blamed on racism, on traditional zoning techniques, on production homebuilding, on television, on air-conditioning, on federal mortgage policies, and above all, on cars. But in examining the global phenomenon, the *Economist* found that a simpler cause transcended all of these factors: "The real cause was mass affluence. As people grew richer, they demanded more privacy and space. Only a few could afford that in city centres; the rest moved out."[8] An international version of the old real estate maxim, "Drive till you qualify."

Few words in modern America are as emotionally freighted as *suburb*. The origin of the term may go back to Cicero, who used it to refer positively to areas outside of Rome in which rich patricians built villas. In medieval times, to live outside the walls of a city was to live in an inferior location—the environs of tanning, industry, and prostitution.[9] From their earliest incarnations, suburbs have been seen as both bad and good.

In America, suburbs became the dominant pattern of settlement after World War II. The portion of people living in suburbs in the United States has grown from 31 percent in 1960 to 51 percent in 2010. And despite a genuine trend toward moving back into the city—chronicled by Leigh Gallagher in *The End of the Suburbs* (2013)—the continued pattern of urbanization in America is increasingly one of suburban form.[10]

From its origin as a simple descriptor of a particular development pattern, *suburb* and its even more loaded derivative, *suburbia*, have become words that prompt strong emotional reactions. Sometimes these reactions are positive: the suburbs continue to signify a lifestyle of choice for people seeking a quiet, comfortable residential enclave, a swimming pool and a backyard, and good schools for the kids. But at least as common is a negative emotional reaction—the suburbs as a land of bland, ticky-tacky sameness; of soulless, mind-numbing conformity.

A rich body of American literature forms a kind of "suburban bashing" genre. Authors like James Howard Kunstler describe the suburbs as soul-sucking, formless, anti-intellectual environments that represent the American dream gone off the rails.[11] Movies like *American Beauty* and *The Truman Show* satirize and critique the plastic nature of life in the suburbs. Popular musicians from Judy Collins to Arcade Fire portray the suburbs as a place for young people to flee in the hope of having a richer and more rewarding life elsewhere.

On the other hand, authors like Joel Kotkin and Robert Bruegmann have articulated a defense of the suburbs as a continuing demographic trend.[12] While the shift of more Americans back toward a higher-density lifestyle is undoubtedly real, it is still relatively small. Both the United States and the rest of the world continue to "suburbanize."

If the term *suburb* has both positive and negative connotations, its companion, *sprawl*, is wholly pejorative. At least since William Whyte's 1958 critique *The Exploding Metropolis*, "urban sprawl" has been a preeminent iconographic image of the negative consequences of postwar American growth.[13] The term *sprawl* serves as an indictment of commercial strip development, of the leapfrog nature of automobile-oriented growth, and of the franchising and nationalizing of retail. Bruegmann's 2003 book *Sprawl: A Compact History* does an excellent job of debunking the notion that sprawl only arrived after World War II. But today the term *sprawl* is inextricably intertwined with auto-dominated city form.

Today there exists a category of American cities in which the line between suburban and urban is almost impossible to locate. These are cities that boomed after World War II based on single-family homes, shopping centers, and the automobile. While such cities have a nominal "downtown," their "sprawling" development pattern long ago outstripped the capacity of that downtown to be the commercial focus for the city's life. These are the new suburban cities of the United States. Though Los Angeles is actually older and became a big city before World War II, it nevertheless serves as a sort of capital of the postwar suburban cities. Others represent a fairly familiar litany of names: Houston, Dallas, Orlando, Jacksonville, Las Vegas, Phoenix.

Any city is, by definition, a concentration of people supported by drawing on a larger geographic resource base. Cities have always been places where farm goods are brought to market. To build any city requires quarrying, mining, and harvesting natural resources from a larger area and transporting them to where people live. Historically, as cities grew larger, the region supporting them expanded. The construction technologies of the late twentieth century raised the relationship of cities and their supporting "resource shed" to a new level. Particularly in the American Southwest, the ability to transport water thousands of miles through canals and pipes and to store it behind huge dams meant that a city could be based on snowfall hundreds of miles away.

The twin hallmarks of the suburban city are the urban fabric built around single-family homes and the automobile, and the need

Figure 1.2. The Central Arizona Project Canal moving Colorado River water through Phoenix. (© Shutterstock: Tim Roberts Photography)

to capture resources from farther and farther away to support an urban population—these two things made such places possible. Yet today, it is these same two factors that lead to the relentless criticism of the suburban city as a kind of giant demographic misstep.

Many commentators dismiss the postwar American city as an unfortunate detour away from higher-density, more traditional urbanism. In this view, the solution to the problems of climate change and more expensive energy is a return to the nineteenth-century city form. This is not an altogether wrong instinct: the postwar American city was built upon cheap petroleum. But we cannot simply abandon the suburban fabric of the last fifty years and wish that things had developed differently.

What happens to these suburban cities in the future? What happens to an urban fabric built not around walking but around driving? What happens to neighborhoods full of large single-family homes as family sizes decline and income levels stagnate? What happens to places that are built upon population growth when

Figure 1.3. Downtown Phoenix. (© Shutterstock: Tim Roberts Photography)

growth slows down? What becomes of cities built in places that are hot and dry as the world turns hotter and drier?

When Jane Jacobs wrote about the death and life of great American cities, she never used the word *sustainability*. Her book was twenty-five years too early for sustainability to be the particular lens through which to examine and critique cities. Today, though, sustainability is *the* filter through which we view the future. To label a place or practice "unsustainable" is to offer a secular damnation of great moment.

In a 2006 radio interview on NPR, author Simon Winchester was discussing his book about the San Francisco earthquake, *A Crack at the Edge of the World*.[14] At the end of his talk, he proposed that there were at least three American cities that "should never have been built": San Francisco because of earthquake faults, New Orleans because of its vulnerability to events like Hurricane Katrina, and

Phoenix because "there's no water there." Winchester's off-the-cuff remarks represented one small effort to analyze the sustainability of American cities. For three completely different reasons, he suggested that three particular cities were so unsustainable they should have never been built in the first place.

The term *sustainability* is generally thought to have originated in the 1987 UN Report *Our Common Future*.[15] Usually referred to as the "Brundtland Report," it defined *sustainability* as "meeting the needs of present generations while not compromising the ability of future generations to meet their own needs." Hosts of other similar formulations are used in order to lend a kind of "I know it when I see it" familiarity to the idea of sustainability. These include: "Don't eat your seed corn"; "Treat the earth as though we intend to stay"; and Gifford Pinchot's description of conservation as "the greatest good for the greatest number for the longest time." Sustainability is sometimes described as three overlapping circles of a Venn diagram where economic performance, social equity, and environmental quality come together and create a sweet spot.

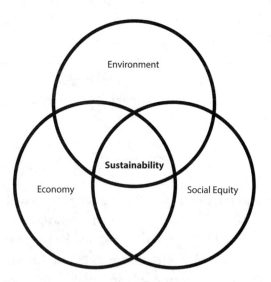

Figure 1.4. The three components of sustainability, with the overlapping "sweet spot."

While these definitions serve well to help capture the intuitive logic of sustainability, it often remains an elusive concept. For example, over what geographic scale is the measurement of "life in balance" supposed to be assessed? Globally? Nationally? Or on a statewide or metropolitan level? Simon Bell and Stephen Morse, in *Measuring Sustainability*, do an admirable job of attempting to catalog the various attempts at creating indices of sustainability or sustainable development.[16] Importantly, they recognize that one of the inherent problems in identifying whether or not a place is sustainable comes from the difficulty in defining what the geography of the "place" actually is. The most logical political geography against which to measure sustainability progress is that of the nation-state. That is, after all, generally where the greatest repository of political power resides, and the nation-state has historically been treated as a discrete functioning society. While the survival of many nation-states depends upon foreign trade, such trade is the subject of treaties and conscious action, unlike the more casual economic interchange between cities or smaller units of government. Since trade at the national level is a subject of explicit policy choices, such choices can be subject to sustainability analysis and influence.

Yet most of the analytical tools developed for measuring and comparing sustainability are aimed at the city or metropolitan level. In the United States this has logical roots, since many of the individual components of sustainability policy are decided locally. There are so many books, monographs, and websites rating the sustainability of cities that there are even multiple reviews of the various rating systems themselves. In most of the scorecards that have been developed, the suburban cities of the American Sunbelt fare poorly.

When Southwestern suburban cities are reviewed, they are often cavalierly dismissed as unsustainable. When the website Gawker.com listed the "Worst States in America," Arizona was rated number one for being an "ecological catastrophe so insanely destructive that they have mist sprayers cooling air even though there is no water there."[17] Sustainlane.com rated the sustainability of cities in 2008. The bottom half of the list essentially ran across the Southwestern Sunbelt: Fort Worth, Dallas, El Paso, Albuquerque, San Diego, Los Angeles, Tucson, Mesa, and Phoenix. At number thirty-two, Phoenix was rated low because its water is moved from far away.[18]

Some more thorough and elaborately designed rankings also reach negative conclusions. On the Siemens Green City Index, Phoenix is twenty-fourth out of twenty-seven American cities.[19] In 2014, when Smart Growth America rated American cities for "sprawl" on a complex four-part matrix, Phoenix came out 173rd and Tucson 171st, with a host of other American Sunbelt cities similarly ranked.[20] Suburban cities are certainly more dependent on the automobile than European and a handful of older American cities. But the Smart Growth America sprawl rankings also have curious anomalies. Phoenix, at number 173, receives a composite score of 78.32. Las Vegas, by contrast, ranks thirty-ninth, with a composite score of 121.20. Yet the two cities are relatively close on individual rankings except with regard to "activity centering." By this measurement, Las Vegas fares well because most people work on the Strip, which is viewed as a "downtown." In Phoenix, on the other hand, jobs are spread throughout the metropolitan area, which actually distributes commuting patterns and lowers overall traffic congestion.

When the consulting firm TetraTech attempted to analyze the risk of climate change to American counties, Maricopa County (Phoenix) appeared near the top of their most-endangered list. Their analysis looked at the difference between rainfall in any given county and the amount of water being used in that county, and then assumed a decrease in rainfall due to climate change. Other Western counties served by large reclamation projects fared similarly in this ranking.[21]

Related to sustainability is the term *resilience*, which is used to refer to the capacity of a place to "bounce back" from any shock or sustainability challenge. Of course, as soon as the term gained currency, ratings of resilience began to appear. One widely used study is the Grosvenor Resilient Cities Research Report, which ranks world cities for vulnerability, adaptive capacity, and resilience.[22] Unfortunately, the Grosvenor Report simply ignores many Sunbelt cities. The US cities in the report include Chicago, Pittsburgh, Boston, Washington, Atlanta, Seattle, New York, Detroit, Los Angeles, and Houston. Los Angeles and Houston fare poorly, far below Detroit or Atlanta. The resilience capacity index rankings used by the University of California rank the Southwestern states generally "low" to "very low" for resilience. Phoenix lands at 233 out of 361 communities—pulled down, most dramatically, by low "community connectivity," a measure of low "rootedness" and high population turnover.

Several themes emerge from the negative rankings of suburban-style American cities. First, cities that are growing tend to be categorized as more challenged and less resilient. This is not surprising, since both physical and social infrastructure tends to lag behind demand in a growing environment. In a stable or shrinking environment, social and physical infrastructure may well have had an opportunity to catch up and in some cases even exceed the demands of a smaller population. Ironically, a place people choose to leave looks more sustainable than one that attracts new residents. So shrinking Detroit wins over booming Houston because there is plenty of excess infrastructure capacity in Detroit.

Second, cities in the arid part of the United States need to draw on a larger external resource base to meet their needs. This is most dramatically the case with regard to water. The downgrading of Western cities because they "move water" from great distances is peculiarly at odds with the history and most of the public policy of such places. Phoenix, for example, was rated below Tucson by Sustainlane because most of its water comes from mountains that are a hundred or more miles distant, or even from the Colorado River. Tucson at the time of this ranking was using a large supply of pumped groundwater. Preferring groundwater is completely counter to Arizona water policy, which encourages the use of renewable surface water rather than finite groundwater.

Kent Portney, in his book *Taking Sustainable Cities Seriously*, notes that with regard to cities one of the common ways of thinking about sustainability is to analyze the ecological footprint of a city: how large an area of resources does it take to support a given concentration of inhabitants?[23] By this measure Phoenix and most of the cities of the arid West have an undeniably large geographic footprint. This is most obvious with regard to water, where—because of aridity and the great hydraulic constructs of the "Reclamation Era"—water is moved long distances to support a population. But saying that Western cities have a large footprint is just another way of saying the arid West has the most concentrated population in the United States—people must live where where resources can be delivered.

In *Power Lines: Phoenix and the Making of the Modern Southwest*, Andrew Needham sees a similar distant exploitation with regard to the generation of electricity. He traces the growth of Phoenix to the enormous concentration of power-generating facilities built in the Four Corners area of the Southwest, fueled by coal from the Black Mesa.[24] This analysis suggests that faraway resources were exploited for the specific purpose of powering a distant civilization, further extending the ecological footprint of Phoenix and other cities.

Portney notes that because the average American citizen needs more than twelve acres of land to support his or her levels of consumption, no city is large enough to allocate that amount of land and therefore no city can be self-sufficient.[25] William Rees notes: "We should remember that cities as presently conceived are incomplete systems typically occupying less than 1 percent of the ecosystem area upon which they draw."[26] This recognition suggests that at anything beyond a village scale, the mere size of a "resource shed" or "ecological footprint" is not a logical measurement of sustainability.

Newer, growing cities often exhibit growing pains in greater social inequality, in volatile economic growth, and in immature political response to challenges. Also, the arid environment of the West, coupled with a semicolonial history of being a region built upon resource extraction, further disadvantages suburban Sunbelt cities in sustainability rankings. Thus, it is not just on environmental metrics that Phoenix and suburban Western cities fare badly. Phoenix, for example, has about 28.5 percent of its population older than twenty-five holding college degrees. That is lower than Atlanta, Denver, Portland, San Diego, Seattle, and Austin. On per capita income the city ranks behind not only most older American cities but is ninth out of ten metro areas that are viewed as relatively direct competitors.[27]

It would be possible to construct a sustainability ranking of cities in which Sunbelt cities would fare better. Such a scale would place greater emphasis on catastrophic sudden natural disasters that cannot be anticipated—and in this many suburban cities would shine. Such a metric would advantage places that store a lot of water rather than rely on local rainfall; that generate a large amount of renewable energy; that do not force all of their citizens to commute to a single location. But constructing such a rating scale is not really the point, and it would serve only to fuel even more alternative rating systems. All cities have challenges of sustainability. Some of these challenges, such as decreasing the use of fossil fuels, are shared. Some challenges, such as enhancing the walkability of urban areas, are greater in some places than others. Some challenges are more unique—coping with the heat island in a place like Phoenix or dealing with sea level rise in New Orleans. Attempting to measure one of these challenges against another and determine which places are more or less sustainable because of specific challenges is interesting and may help to illuminate specific issues, but at the end of the day it is probably a relatively fruitless exercise that is unlikely to determine the actual likelihood that a particular place will survive.

As a result of the difficulty of comparing places with vastly different geographies and histories, a number of sustainability rankings shift instead to an alternative method of reviewing the degree to which a particular jurisdiction adopts sustainability practices.

It is relatively easy to assess which city is doing better on recycling or on growing food locally, or who has more farmers' markets, or which city is moving more quickly to build LEED-certified buildings. (As of 2012, the EPA rated Phoenix ninth for most Energy Star buildings, ahead of Boston, Seattle, and Portland.) These comparisons result not in analyzing the long-term sustainability of one place versus another but rather in comparing the current policy choices being made in one place versus another. This can be valuable analysis, for often by realizing that better policy choices are being made somewhere else we can prompt different choices closer to home. Competition is always a motivating choice for political bodies.

Figure 1.5. The Tempe Transportation Center is a LEED Platinum building that serves as the main transit hub for Tempe and contains municipal and private offices, a conference center, a restaurant, and a bike storage and repair facility. (Photo by author)

Portney thus concludes that one view of a sustainable city is whether it is *attempting* to become more sustainable. An analysis of trajectory rather than of status leads most efforts to grade the sustainability of cities to becoming efforts at analyzing the number, quality, or efficacy of a city's sustainability programs: how seriously do cities take sustainability? These ratings are based on scores of water policy, waste disposal, land-use management, and transportation decisions, as well as the extent to which individual city policies at least appear to be grounded in sustainability principles. Portney's 2011 rankings of the sustainability score of the fifty-five largest cities in the United States has Phoenix tied for number seven, along with Chicago, Minneapolis, and Philadelphia. Albuquerque, another Sunbelt city, is at number five, with Denver number four. Tucson is tied at number sixteen with Charlotte and Austin. By these measures—how seriously a city is taking challenges of sustainability—Sunbelt cities fare much better.[28] Perhaps this is evidence that newer cities recognize they may have different and urgent challenges. Or perhaps a faster-growing place feels more compelled to anticipate likely problems.

Under its last two mayors, Phoenix has made a major effort to move city policies toward sustainability. In 2009, former Mayor Phil Gordon announced an intention to make Phoenix "the greenest city in America." Under current mayor Greg Stanton, the city has appointed a sustainability officer and moved dramatically toward looking at its own practices and behaviors with regard to energy consumption and facility management. The Las Vegas City Council started articulating aggressive sustainability goals in 2008, even proposing efforts to become the first "net zero" city in America.[29]

Interestingly, even one of Phoenix's most articulate critics, Andrew Ross, found great hope in the city's attempts to cope with challenges. His book *Bird on Fire* is a classic example of an Eastern observer looking askance at an odd place he does not really understand. His book begins with the classic demonizing of dwelling where it does not rain very much. But rather than actually attempting to defend his subtitle (*The World's Least Sustainable City*), he simply says: "Even if it is not the world's least sustainable city (and some will quibble over this designation), it is a very close contender and in any event the title is not worth arguing over."[30] After extensively reviewing the environmental, social, and political challenges of Phoenix, at the end of the book Ross seems to have at least moderate hope for Phoenix:

> More susceptible, or recalcitrant, places have other things to teach us—how we go about making green decisions or whether we even have the wherewithal to make the right ones. That is why I chose to write this book about the struggle to make Phoenix into a resilient metropolis. Faced with larger environmental challenges, and considerably more resistance from elected officials than havens of green consciousness like Seattle or San Francisco, it is a more accurate bellwether of sustainability than these success stories.[31]

It is certainly valuable to compare one city with another in order to analyze whether behavior can be modified. It is surely useful to hold up political decision making against a standard that requires politicians and bureaucrats to care about the future. But the real measure of whether a given place can survive over the very long term is how well that place has dealt in the past with specific challenges and how likely it is to be able to continue to do so.

The criticism of the suburban cities of the American West as unsustainable is principally grounded in looking at a set of challenges that older American cities and the historic cities of Western Europe did not face. These are the challenges of being hot and dry, of being designed around automobiles, and of having boom-and-bust economies built on high mobility. These specific attributes of the suburban American city pose the question of sustainability that must be examined in thinking about the survival of such places.

Are suburban cities sustainable? It's not a simple question, but one that is too often brushed off with a cavalierly simple answer— "No." The casual dismissal of suburban cities as unsustainable because of "sprawl" is not supportable, though it does represent an understandable, if biased, instinct. Places that grew up based on the automobile and the single-family home need to change and evolve dramatically. Just as pre-automobile cities had to readjust their urban fabric and density in response to the automobile, so the suburban cities of America will need to adapt to future changes. The difference is that in the twenty-first century change and adaptation will happen at an ever-faster pace.

The overlap between suburban cities and the cities of the arid West is huge, for the growth curves coincided: America's western migration accelerated simultaneously with the dominance of the automobile and the single-family home. So cities like Phoenix are doubly condemned—both dry and sprawling. The impulse to view cities of the arid West as unsustainable in the face of climate change is similarly simplistic—and not fully supportable. Such cities were built based on great plumbing systems that move water long distances. The availability of that water is stoutly challenged. These challenges will force adaptation and tough choices with regard to the survival of agriculture, the nature of landscape, and the behavior of human populations. Yet the ability to move water remains, and the supplies, though challenged, are not going to simply vanish altogether.

Supplying the water necessary to support a big city in a dry place has been the central dilemma of cities like Phoenix ever since their birth. It is not realistic to assume that a challenge that has been met again and again in the past suddenly represents an insurmountable barrier.

Sunbelt suburban cities, which became comfortable places to live only when air-conditioning was an available technology, will undoubtedly be challenged by what we used to call "global warming." In Phoenix, an ever-hotter future is not attractive. There are days when the place already seems uninhabitable. To imagine it seven or ten degrees Fahrenheit hotter is almost unthinkable. One aspect of such heat is a local phenomenon called the "heat island" effect, which scientists and urban planners in metropolitan Phoenix and other hot-weather cities are studying and finding ways to mitigate. Some aspects of climate change that are likely to increase maximum temperatures are not rooted in local, and therefore locally manageable, causes. The global impact of greenhouse gases on maximum temperatures will have to be accommodated through increased reliance on the technologies of air-conditioning, construction, and landscaping. Again, though, to assume that high temperatures represent an insurmountable obstacle for places like Phoenix belies the history of dealing with such a challenge. It is easier to accommodate steadily rising high temperatures than rising sea level or extraordinary natural events like tornadoes and hurricanes.

Suburban cities are recognizing the need to modify the pattern of their built environments in both transportation and land-use changes. Los Angeles, Phoenix, Denver, Salt Lake City, Las Vegas, and a host of other suburban cities have expanded public transit opportunities, and in many cases have built rail systems, as alternatives to automobile travel. These transportation changes both react to and provoke changes in land-use patterns. Increasingly, consumers are choosing to live at higher densities and with less reliance on the automobile. The continued evolution of work away from being tethered to an individual factory or office is already beginning to profoundly alter the built environment and the transportation dynamic of all American cities.

Into this evolutionary stew, a once Jetsons-like fantasy is rapidly becoming real: not flying cars but driverless cars. The prospect of driverless vehicles, which will be smaller and lighter than traditional automobiles, and likely not powered by internal combustion

Figure 1.6. Los Angeles has multiple rail systems. MetroRail started service in 1990 and serves nearly 500,000 riders daily. (Source: LA Metro, https://www.metro.net)

engines, is becoming real so quickly as to be almost incomprehensible. Transportation on demand and purchased only as needed will almost certainly help preserve and sustain the suburban city lifestyle.

So is the suburban city sustainable? Is Phoenix, Arizona, sustainable? Answer: probably, so long as it maintains the ability to change and adapt at an ever-faster pace.

Chapter 2

Just Add Water

THE LAST TIME ONE STATE BRANDISHED arms against another was in 1934. The issue was water. Arizona Governor B. B. Moeur dispatched his executive assistant and 102 members of the Arizona National Guard to a godforsaken spot on the Arizona side of the Colorado River south of Parker. Armed with machine guns, rifles, and tear gas bombs, their mission was to dislodge four one-inch-thick cables that California had connected to the Arizona side to begin the construction of Parker Dam. The dam would divert water from the river into the proposed California Aqueduct. The Arizona troops commandeered two ferryboats, and the whole affair was written up in the *Los Angeles Times* as the hilarious misadventure of the Arizona Navy.[1]

Among the factors of urban growth in the Southwest, water is the most storied, the most litigated, the most complex. To grow food and sustain human life, four basic ingredients are necessary:

sun, air, water, and land. Of these, only water is easily portable. In central Arizona, this fact was first recognized by the Hohokam, who built an elaborate irrigation system that provided water to hundreds of thousands of acres by the year 1415. Spanish settlement in New Mexico likewise congregated around water systems.

In 2008, when one national group ranked the sustainability of American cities for water supply, it used as its primary measure how far water is transported.[2] Not surprisingly, Phoenix ranked number forty-nine out of fifty. Indeed, water is transported long distances to support Phoenix. On the other hand, until recent years, Tucson existed primarily on mined groundwater, so it was rated by this same source as "more sustainable." Yet Arizona's water policy for more than thirty years has been to try to wean cities from using the nonrenewable resource of groundwater and instead to build on renewable surface water supplies. Moving surface water to urban use is an official early-policy example of shifting to more "sustainable" practices. This distinction is embedded in Arizona's Groundwater Management Act and a host of other policy decisions.

Balmier places have taken for granted that their hospitable climate will continue into the future, so a place like Atlanta is greatly challenged when rainfall decreases by 15 or 20 percent. Phoenix, on the other hand, hardly depends at all on rainfall occurring within its geographic proximity. Phoenix's water comes primarily from the mountains of central Arizona (delivered through the Salt River Project) and from the Rockies (transported through the Colorado River and the Central Arizona Project). Together, these two sources can generally deliver about 2 million acre-feet of water to the Phoenix metro area (an acre-foot is about 325,000 gallons, approximately two urban households' annual use in Phoenix).[3]

Versions of the large watering systems that support central Arizona are found throughout the arid West, a legacy of the "reclamation era," when the federal government subsidized settlement by constructing massive water-moving plumbing in order to encourage agriculture and ultimately city building. It is important to understand this history when considering why arid-region cities draw their water from distant sources. The story of moving water in the Western United States to places where people live exemplifies how cities draw on a larger area for their resources. Understanding that history gives context to the current drought and guides our thinking about that drought in analyzing the sustainability of places like Phoenix.

An irony of living in the West, with its culture of purported "rugged individualism," is that the need to find water leads to cooperative behavior in settlement building. The coming together of people who benefit from water distributed through ditches is the Southwestern equivalent of a New England barn raising. Cooperation among settlers is required, so the earliest forms of government in arid regions tend to be those that deal with water: the *acequia*, the water district, the ditch company.

At some point, an entire settlement's cooperation is insufficient to deal with water needs, and the assistance of "outsiders" becomes necessary. In Phoenix, this first occurred in 1883 when William J. Murphy, a railroad contractor, was hired to begin work on the Arizona Canal, a large ditch planned to run through lands the Hohokam had never irrigated on the northern edge of the Valley.[4] But the "outsider" most important to Phoenix was the United States government.

Early on, John Wesley Powell recognized the need for the federal government to play a major role in Western water issues. Powell proposed to close the public domain to the spotty settlement that was taking place and instead organize vast areas of the West along geographical lines following hydrological basins within which all of the natural resources would be tied together by the controlling element of water.[5] Water should form the basis for planning Western growth and settlement.

The West of the 1880s was already too settled for Powell's sweeping vision to be accepted. Most settlement had begun, in places like Phoenix, on the basis of immediate proximity to water. When the local supply proved inadequate, existing investments in land made it preferable to search for new water sources rather than to move. Instead of a grand scheme to manage hydrologic basins and plan development accordingly, water was a commodity that entrepreneurs sought to transport to where they had already established a toehold.

Local recognition of the need for cooperative efforts and outside assistance in managing water supplies often came in times of crisis. In the case of Phoenix, a "perfect storm" of maladies did the trick. The droughts of 1898 and 1899 forced a third of the valley's 200,000 acres of irrigated farmland out of cultivation; in 1890, a flood burst the Walnut Grove Dam on the Hassayampa River, killing sixty people or more; water reached downtown Phoenix in an 1891 flood.[6]

Modern Arizona's reliance on great water projects dates to these events at the turn of the twentieth century. The initial settlers had seen a vision in the remains of the prehistoric canal system and had begun reconstructing it in order to take advantage of the agricultural potential of the area. Initially, their canals simply diverted flow directly from the Salt River as it went through town—an unreliable method. The early history of those canals is a tale of intrigue, fraud, and even armed conflict. The right to water was often transferred with shares in the canal company, rather than with the land being irrigated. The situation was a mess of conflicting priorities and shady legal claims for far more water than actually existed.[7]

When it was passed in 1902, the Newlands Reclamation Act established the Reclamation Service and authorized a variety of water projects throughout the West. The Salt River Valley Water Users Association (SRVWUA) was formed, and in 1903 it succeeded in obtaining authorization for Roosevelt Dam sixty miles from Phoenix at the confluence of Tonto Creek and the Salt River.

Upon its completion in 1911, Roosevelt Dam was the largest masonry dam in the world, creating what was then the largest

Figure 2.1. Roosevelt Dam impounded the Salt River, making modern Phoenix possible. (© Shutterstock: Barry Singleton)

artificial lake in the world. The Salt River Project (SRP) was the first multipurpose reclamation project in the country in that it generated hydroelectric power, delivered water, and provided flood protection to Phoenix. (SRVWUA ultimately became part of SRP.) When former President Theodore Roosevelt dedicated the dam named after him in 1911, he predicted that central Arizona would become "one of the richest agricultural areas in the world."[8]

When the Salt River Valley began to urbanize, formerly irrigated agricultural fields became subdivisions. Prior to 1948, only 22,000 acres of farmland had been subdivided, but the following decade saw the development of another 32,000 acres.[9] In most cases, these new urbanizing areas used less water than had the previous agricultural users, so the conversion did not strain the water systems.

Even prior to Governor Moeur and the "Arizona Navy," generations of Arizona politicians had made Arizona's right to waters from the Colorado River an article of faith never to be questioned.

Figure 2.2. Water being delivered for irrigated agriculture in central Arizona. (© Shutterstock: Jim Parkin)

Besides, once the Salt River had been harnessed, there was nowhere else to turn. Additional water was necessary in order to continue growing both cities and crops, and the quest for this water became a recognized community goal. Arizonans believed they should be entitled to the biggest piece of the Colorado's water because the river flows through or is adjacent to the state for almost half of its length and is fed by a number of tributaries flowing from Arizona. California, by contrast, contributes very little water to the flow of "the river." But California had a strong claim based on a historic pattern of agricultural use in the Imperial Valley and a large population with great political power. The so-called basin states are those of the upper basin (Colorado, Wyoming, Utah, and New Mexico) and the lower basin (Nevada, Arizona, and California). Most of the water comes from snowmelt in the Rockies, giving the upper basin the rationale for their claims. Most is *used* in the lower basin, especially in California, a long-standing historical claim.

In 1922, the US Supreme Court ruled that the state of Colorado could not assert the right to all of the water arising within its boundaries, making the division of its waters among the seven basin states and Mexico legally possible.[10] This would be accomplished by building the largest dam the world had ever seen in Boulder Canyon. The apportionment of the water was set by the signing of the Colorado River Compact in Santa Fe on November 25, 1922. Arizona opposed ratification of the compact and most of the local residents saw it as another plot to steal water, because the agreement allotted California 4.4 million acre-feet but only 2.8 million acre-feet to Arizona. Although Arizona refused to ratify the Colorado River Compact for decades, the state finally came to the realization that it was better to fight for federal help to build the necessary works to use the water it had been allocated rather than to assert its claims for more.[11]

Nevada, which at the time had few people, no farming, and only touched the river briefly, got only 300,000 acre-feet. The growth of Las Vegas, a city originally based on easy divorce and later on dreams of easy riches, was unanticipated. Hence, of all the cities in the arid West, Las Vegas now faces the greatest challenges to find sufficient water to survive.

In January 1963, Floyd Dominy, legendary head of the US Bureau of Reclamation, together with Secretary of the Interior (and Arizonan) Stewart Udall, announced the biggest water project ever: pumping Colorado River water out of Lake Havasu to central Arizona. In 1968, the Central Arizona Project (CAP) authorization was signed by President Lyndon Johnson. To Arizona, the price of this legislation was high: California got its full 4.4 million acre-feet allocation guaranteed as a priority, a right that is senior to Arizona's.[12]

When Jimmy Carter was elected president in 1976, one of his earliest actions was to release a list of Western water projects that he proposed to cut, including the CAP. In order to save it, Secretary of the Interior Cecil Andrus exacted a price: since the state was seriously depleting its groundwater resources, the CAP would only

Figure 2.3. The Central Arizona Project (CAP) is designed to bring approximately 1.5 million acre-feet of Colorado River water annually to Pima, Pinal, and Maricopa Counties. (© Shutterstock: Tim Roberts Photography)

be funded if the state passed pumping limitations.[13] As a result, in 1980 the Groundwater Management Act (GMA), one of the most sweeping pieces of legislation in Arizona history, was passed. In fact, Andrus's threat did Arizona a favor: California was unable to pass any groundwater pumping limitations until 2014. Limiting groundwater pumping is seen as an incursion on property rights by long-standing pumpers. But an aquifer doesn't respect lot lines, and the cumulative impact of unlimited pumping is as clear a manifestation of the tragedy of the commons as one can imagine—water levels decline, quality suffers, land may subside, and everyone is damaged. Some level of regulation is ultimately needed to protect the aquifer.

The GMA meant a new role for the state in administering Arizona's water resources. The Department of Water Resources (DWR) was created to oversee the administration of the Active Management Areas (AMA) and to issue certificates ensuring a 100-year water supply for subdivisions before land could be sold. In practice, this would force most new development in metropolitan areas to be annexed into existing municipalities.

In the arid West, the past dialogue about urban water has not been about quality of life, long-range growth, or development form. Arizona's tribal imperative is too strong: we need all the water we can get and we will do anything we can to fight anyone who challenges that assumption. Because the absence of water is the defining characteristic of a desert, the management of water becomes the defining activity of life in the desert. The thirst for water supplies has been the initial organizing force for most major desert communities, including Phoenix, and once people have banded together to fight for water resources, the ongoing acquisition of that resource becomes the unifying ethic—and the most unquestionable goal of government. Controlling water and agreeing to share it defines "us." Others become "them."

Another reality of water in the desert is that, after acquisition, delivery is the central problem. The infrastructure cost to develop water is very high and, as a result, "from plumbing flows policy." Only major government action, usually by the federal government, makes it possible to absorb such costs. The plumbing necessary to deliver water in support of people means that development in the desert is a phenomenon of concentration. A desert dweller cannot simply settle wherever he wants, drill a shallow and cheap well, and set up a subsistence farm. He needs access to communal systems.

John Wesley Powell's vision of centralized planning, controlled settlement, and community-held assets was too collective and too socialistic to be acceptable to Westerners. To implement Powell's plan would have meant concluding that most of the arid West would never be suitable for habitation. Making such sweeping and discriminatory judgments at a government level was no more popular then than it would be now. But the failure to plan the growth of the arid West around such restrictions has meant instead that growth is structured around the giant plumbing systems that move, concentrate, and redistribute water over vast distances. The economic realities of building such systems have had profound impacts on urban form, imposing to a great degree what would have been difficult to accept by government mandate: most of the West will remain undeveloped.

Desert cities tend to exist in concentrated isolation—wholly unlike the pattern of widely spread towns, farms, and small settlements in the Midwest or East. Leapfrog development generally cannot leap very far in a desert environment. There are few truly rural areas on the borders of a desert city. Even farming in the desert is a phenomenon of concentration, both economically (in the hands of large commercial interests that can manage delivery systems) and also geographically (in areas where watercourses are built). In central Arizona, the bubble of urbanization is big, but its outline is distinct. Urban settlement either runs right up to vacant desert, as in north Scottsdale, Las Vegas, or Tucson; or, as on the west side of Phoenix or in the East Valley near Mesa, there may be a mile or two of farmland as a buffer between the urban edge and the desert.

The serious drought that has gripped the West since 2010 is stressing the watering systems that were created during the twentieth century. California's situation is the most dire. The magnitude of the crisis has been made clear by negative publicity about the plight of California agriculture, as well as by emergency efforts of the governor and legislature to regulate groundwater pumping and cut back urban water use.

Central Arizona's position as a junior right holder to Colorado River water, with California senior, and the simple fact that Arizona looks so much drier and generally receives less annual average rainfall than California (not to mention that it has no nearby ocean) have led many national commentators to the conclusion that the drought surely will be significantly worse news for Arizona. The headline of an article on *Slate* (May 8, 2015) was "Yes, the Drought Is Bad in California, but It's Going to Be Much, Much Worse in Arizona."[14]

Arizona's director of the Department of Water Resources and a host of other Arizona elected officials up to and including the new governor have tried valiantly to explain to the national press that Arizona is actually in a much better position than California, but they have had a hard time getting any attention.

There are a number of critical differences between Arizona and California with regard to drought preparation:

1. California's systems are far more dependent on annual precipitation than are Arizona's. Because Arizona's annual precipitation is so low, the state has always presumed that there will be little rainfall. While precipitation has declined, the shift is not nearly as dramatic as in California, which assumed a higher rate of annual rainfall.

2. Arizona began regulating groundwater pumping in 1980 with the Groundwater Management Act. While those regulations are far from perfect and, in some cases, have not been as successful as hoped, they have resulted in overall declines in pumping. The rate of overdraft in Arizona's Active Management Areas has declined over 90 percent since the passage of the GMA.

3. For nearly twenty years, Arizona has been engaged in a strenuous program of banking water in its underground aquifers. As of mid-2015, nearly 9 million acre-feet of water have been stored in the "Sun Corridor," the name given to the Phoenix-Tucson urban region of central Arizona. That represents about 3 trillion gallons, or nearly a decade's worth of urban water. This water was stored with the explicit goal of being ready for declarations of shortage on the Colorado River. Recognizing Arizona's junior status as a claimant to Colorado River water, in times of plenty the state began banking water to pull back up when a shortage is declared. "Shortage" does not mean

zero deliveries, so the banked water can be used over a very long time period.

4. California's agricultural users have very senior and very direct rights to Colorado River water. This results in California facing difficult confrontations when the need arises to move that water away from agriculture to urban uses. Despite this, California has had some success in bargains being reached between the cities and agricultural interests. In Arizona, agriculture along the river in Yuma and La Paz Counties has similar very senior rights. But the agriculture served by the Central Arizona Project surrendered longtime rights to water in exchange for a reduction in the price of water after the CAP canal was declared complete. This allows water deliveries to CAP-based agriculture in central Arizona to be cut back in times of drought, with more water being delivered to cities.

5. In the past fifty years, urban development in Arizona has replaced agricultural use. The conversion of farms to houses, so characteristic of Phoenix's growth, has actually decreased overall water use, as subdivisions use less water than farms. It has also meant that agricultural uses have transitioned relatively smoothly to urban use. As a result, the state uses today about the same water it did in 1957, but with nearly ten times as many people.

6. Arizona agriculture is among the most efficient in the nation. In the CAP service area, the agricultural community has exceeded the state's 80 percent water-efficiency target through the lining of canals, laser-leveling of fields, conversion from flood irrigation to sprinkler and drip systems, and use of automated real-time delivery. In Yuma, irrigation efficiency rates are even higher.[15]

7. Similarly, in the last couple of decades, Arizona homeowners have been able to curtail per capita consumption. This has been done primarily through education, resulting in a shift away from grass and lush trees toward xeriscaping. The smaller lots and higher densities of recent developments in the Phoenix area have also curtailed per capita water use.

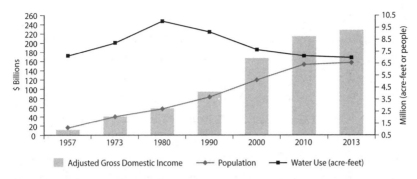

Figure 2.4. Arizona water use, population, and economic growth (1957–2013). (Source: Arizona Department of Water Resources)

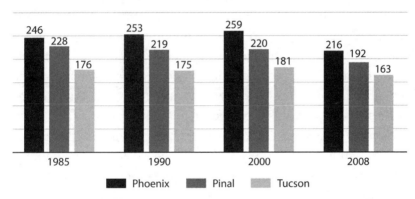

Figure 2.5. Rates of daily water usage, in gallons per capita per day, for Central Arizona AMAs. (Source: Arizona Department of Water Resources)

The reality that Arizona is better off than California is testament to Arizona's deep, long-term, consistent commitment to recognizing water as the central challenge of living in the desert. Throughout Arizona's history, water has been the thing that Arizona understood the best, cared about the most, and worked at the hardest, giving the state a margin of resilience and protection in times of drought. In 2011, Arizona State University's Morrison Institute issued a report called *Watering the Sun Corridor* that looked at the growth of the

Phoenix-Tucson urban area and sought to extrapolate from current trends in order to determine the carrying capacity of that area from a water-supply perspective. Even if climate change decreases water supply by 25 percent or more, the storage systems serving Phoenix and the Sun Corridor hold years' worth of water and are designed to smooth out a highly variable supply. More than half of the Sun Corridor's water supply is used for agriculture. *Watering the Sun Corridor* concludes that, even under worst-case climate assumptions, with moderately increased conservation and a steady decline in agriculture the Sun Corridor could accommodate several million additional people.[16]

Today, the Morrison Institute's 2011 assumptions look as though they may be too optimistic. The continued severity and length of the drought and increasingly dire predictions about the impact of climate change appear to suggest an even greater reduction in assumed supply. Sustaining Phoenix requires a lot of water. As Table 2.1 shows, per capita water usage in Phoenix is the second highest of the nation's fifteen most populous metropolitan areas. This placement should not be surprising; the region's arid climate and hot summers naturally lead to higher average consumption, primarily because water is used to support landscaping.

Aridity is a challenge—but it is not a challenge like a hurricane. Hurricanes are periodic catastrophic events that can, at best, be anticipated by a few days, or if forecasting improves, a few weeks. They are events with potentially dire, immediate, sudden consequences. While it is possible to take steps that will mitigate the impact of such catastrophes, they occur quickly and often must be managed after the fact by way of emergency response. A drought, on the other hand, even in the worst of circumstances, is a slowly unfolding, largely incremental change to climate. Urban Arizona's vast and complex plumbing systems are a perfect example of man's capacity to manage resources against such challenges. Growth and the potential of a further drying of the American Southwest will pose new and incrementally greater challenges to these systems.

Table 2.1. Water Usage per Capita in the Fifteen Most Populous Metro Areas of the United States

Metropolitan Area	Gallons per Person per Day
New York	69.3
Boston	73.5
Atlanta	121.9
Seattle	127.7
Philadelphia	134.4
San Francisco	142.0
Chicago	144.8
Washington	149.5
Charlotte	153.3
Houston	158.4
Detroit	172.3
Miami	172.6
Denver	181.2
Los Angeles	187.0
Phoenix	217.3
Dallas	219.3

Source: USGS, 2005 (as reported in the Green City Index, 2011).

This is already under way, and the result has been the replacement of agricultural use with subdivisions, a steady increase in water prices, and a dramatic reduction in per capita water use.

Arizona's careful long-term commitment to thinking about water is the best example it can offer to other places as they consider long-term resource challenges. Water needs to be carefully managed against future assumptions, and in this it resembles a family's financial circumstances. How much do you need to keep in easily available savings in order to deal with a sudden unexpected catastrophe? How much are you willing to compromise your current lifestyle in order to sustain that lifestyle in an uncertain future? Should you be willing to tap your inheritance (in this case, groundwater) if your cash flow (or renewable water supply) is suddenly diminished? How much do you need to leave for future generations? These are the policy choices of sustainability. But unlike family finances, water decisions are made by a city, state, or other political entity.

While Arizona has done well with regard to water management, a number of major challenges loom. These are not simply challenges of the immediate drought. Rather, the growth of the western United States has reached the point at which, even without a drought, the water systems are overtaxed. Systems originally built to encourage agriculture have continued to supply agriculture even as cities have grown larger and larger. As a result, water use in the West is running on a deficit basis. In metropolitan Phoenix and the Sun Corridor, a number of conversations are under way about this reality. Some of those conversations center on the possibility of augmenting water supply through cloud seeding or desalinization. But on a more immediate basis, the talk is of making choices between different uses of water. These conversations are harbingers of dialogues that must take place throughout many urban areas.

The first water-related issues that must be faced in an arid urban location are figuring out who has the right to how much water. Until the competing demands for water can be sorted out and quantified, it is difficult to progress to conversations about either greater conservation or augmenting supply.

Throughout the West, water rights have generally been awarded based on the doctrine of prior appropriation: "First in time, first in right." That was a policy explicitly created to incentivize settling an empty, dry place. By giving rights to the first people who would take the initiative to go out and attempt to live in a desert, the legal system created expectations that resulted in luring people into the country "beyond the hundredth meridian." It was a policy that worked—that arid region is now one of the most urbanized parts of the country. In many ways, the doctrine of prior appropriation probably no longer makes sense. But now huge investments, largely by agricultural users, have been made on the basis of that doctrine. Accordingly, legal change in this area must happen slowly in order to protect the investment-backed expectations of generations of Western settlers. Figuring out how to adapt long-term water-rights expectations that arose in a context very different from today's world is one of the serious challenges facing the western United States.

Sorting the competing demands for water is particularly difficult in Arizona. For generations Arizona has separated water into two theoretically distinct commodities: groundwater and surface water. The system created in Arizona is based on the hydrological fiction that there is little or no relationship between water underground and water flowing in a stream. This distinction has begun to break down in a series of forty-year-old court cases, still in litigation, concerning when groundwater pumping impacts a flowing river.[17] To litigate for forty years is, by definition, counterproductive. Yet these "general stream adjudications" grind on slowly. In order to make progress toward a new era of water planning, the adjudications must be resolved and a conclusion quantifying water rights must be reached before new, more robust water management systems can be created. As of early 2015, a newly formed unit at Arizona State University, the Kyl Center for Water Policy, was attempting to find a means of hastening these long-term adjudications.

Regardless of whether the adjudicated water rights of Arizona can be substantially clarified, the urban Sun Corridor must come further to grips with how water is used. In the early part of the twenty-first century, the Sun Corridor was still using about two-thirds of its water for commercial agricultural operations and about one-third for urban populations. It is this reality that gives rise to Arizona water managers' sense that there is sufficient water supply to sustain the urban populations of central Arizona far into the future. After all, the history of urbanizing in Arizona has been one of moving water from farms to cities. For a variety of reasons, though, those assumptions are now being revisited.

First, it is quite clear that the long-term sustainable water supply of the entire Colorado River Basin is simply not what it was once believed to be. Mistakes were made when the river was originally allocated. The "law of the river"—the complex web of treaties, acts of Congress, compacts, and adjudications—assumed a reliable flow of the Colorado of about 17.5 million acre-feet. That flow was split between the upper basin and lower basin states and Mexico. Today, extensive research in tree-ring analysis, primarily by the University of Arizona, leads to the conclusion that the actual reliable flow of the river is significantly less, maybe only in the 12- to 13-million acre-foot range.[18]

Second, even the scientific estimates of the actual historical flow rate of the river have been challenged; it is likely declining from climate change.[19] Third, the demands put upon the Colorado River, and indeed upon all of the waters in the western United States, are changing, becoming increasingly urban in character. Urban water demands are "hard," meaning much less susceptible to management in times of drought. Simply put, it is easier to cut back water deliveries to a farm than it is to a single-family home.

A fourth reality is that the Sun Corridor occupies a low priority in receiving water from the Colorado—a price the State of Arizona had to pay for the federal government's agreement to fund the Central Arizona Project. In addition, the portion of the Sun Corridor's water supply that comes from the mountains of central Arizona, delivered through the Salt River Project, is under increasing stress from the urbanization of the recreational areas of north-central Arizona. Here, the residents of Phoenix seek to escape the oppressive summer heat by building high-elevation retreats, which means that they are in the mountains competing for the same water supplies that they have been consuming in the desert.

The combination of all of these factors means that the demands for water in the growing part of urban Arizona will continue to be put under greater and greater stress, forcing tough choices to be made about whether and to what extent agriculture should be preserved in central Arizona. In *Watering the Sun Corridor*, the Morrison Institute posited a probable 2.4 million acre-foot "supply assumption" for the Sun Corridor as a relatively reliable annual input to the water system, given an assumed 15 percent reduction in flow due to climate change. It might be appropriate to make an even greater reduction to accommodate the likely risk of climate change, down to perhaps something in the 2-million acre-foot range. At that level, if all agriculture in the Sun Corridor were eliminated and if everyone who lived in the area consumed 200 gallons per capita per day (which is about the current average), the population of the Sun Corridor could be 9 million people. A decrease in per capita use down to 150 gallons per capita per day (GPCD), which is an attainable number still far in excess of what cities in the arid portions of Australia now use, would allow a population of about 12 million people.

Very few Western cities can point to an available water supply that can support future growth to the degree that the communities of metropolitan Phoenix can. In Los Angeles, San Diego, Las Vegas, Albuquerque, Santa Fe, and even Denver, water supply imposes more immediate limits to population growth.

Running out of water is not imminent. Nor is it conceivable that residents of the Sun Corridor will turn on their taps and have nothing come out. The existing vast plumbing systems, storage mechanisms, and redundant supplies are all designed to protect urban domestic use as the paramount water demand. But how to use water is—and will remain—the defining challenge of the place. The question ultimately becomes: How much should Sun Corridor residents adjust their lifestyle and uses of water to accommodate more residents? Using less water per capita will change the way people live. It will also mean that the water supply can be stretched further. This essential tension manifests itself in numerous policy choices.

Agriculture. The simplest explanation of Phoenix and the Sun Corridor's relatively comfortable water situation is that more than half of the available water is used to grow crops. That huge amount can potentially be rededicated to urban populations and can, therefore, support long-term growth. The assumption has been that the growing region's future water supply will come from the gradual transfer of water from agriculture to urban uses. But shifting from the former to the latter "hardens" the demand. In other parts of the country, preserving local agricultural suppliers is a pressing matter of sustainability, healthy lifestyles, historic cultures, land use and open-space preservation, and anti-globalization trends. All of these issues deserve greater discussion in the Sun Corridor, but the issue of water management flexibility is far more important.

Suppose, for example, that 500,000 acre-feet of water is permanently used for farming. This policy choice is likely to be made by central Arizona's tribal communities. The Gila River Indian Community is receiving a large share of CAP water in settlement of its ancient claims. Most of that share is intended to be used for farming on their reservation between Phoenix and Tucson. At an average use of 150 GPCD, such a water allocation would mean 2.9 million fewer people can be accommodated in the future.

Economic Development. What kind of an economy should be supported by Western water supplies? How does water use support or limit economic choices? Electronics manufacturing, still a staple of the Phoenix economy, uses a lot of water, but it does so efficiently and adds high economic value. Growing alfalfa uses a lot of water and has relatively low economic value. Golf courses use a great deal of water, but if coupled with resort hotels, they are a mainstay of tourism, which "imports" dollars into the area. Solar power is presently part of the state's economic development strategy, but some kinds of solar power generation are water intensive. Expanded copper mining—it was, of course, a preeminent reason for Arizona's early existence as a state—uses a lot of water, often in ways that are not fully accounted for in GPCD projections.

Generally, land-use decisions and economic-development decisions have been completely divorced from water decisions.

Communities make a rezoning decision or decide to incentivize the creation of new jobs, and subsequently the water department is expected to find water for whatever use has been approved. In the early summer of 2015, the City of Chandler, which has long been a leader among Arizona municipalities on water issues, adopted a novel policy of explicitly reserving some of its excess water supply for use in responding to particular alternative developments in the future.[20] Should this water be used to grow more subdivisions? Or would it be better—more economically advantageous to the city—to apply it to a new electronics manufacturing plant? Maybe a golf course in connection with a large resort catering to tourism? Or maybe a water-based amusement park? The decision to begin to link those decisions with the use of water was driven largely by the realization that Chandler was becoming a global Mecca for large data centers—huge, windowless warehouses filled by racks and racks of computers that make up a part of the cyberspace "cloud." Chandler, Arizona, came to realize that the data centers were consuming significant amounts of water for air-conditioning but providing very few jobs. Maybe, Chandler city officials thought, there would be a better way to use water that would have otherwise gone automatically to such purposes. The city's mechanism is to set an expected water budget for uses identified in its general plan. As projects actually come in for approval requesting water in excess of the water budget, the city council can choose either to draw from the discretionary pool or to tell a user that it must find its own additional water.

Where Should Growth Occur? Like everywhere in the arid West, all parts of the Sun Corridor are not equal. The big cities of the Phoenix metropolitan area, especially those parts within the boundaries of the Salt River Project, have the largest, most reliable, and most flexible water supplies. Much recent growth has taken place in smaller municipalities on the west side and in the high-growth mid-Corridor geography of Pinal County. Over the long term, this may not be the most sustainable growth pattern. Either new (and potentially less reliable) water supplies will be needed to support urbanizing areas, or existing supplies will have to flow toward development, or development will need to migrate to areas with firmer supplies. This may well produce a clash between market forces pushing homebuilding toward the fringe, and legal and institutional protections of existing water rights pushing additional development back into older neighborhoods.

Density. If development is to move where the most reliable supplies are, the existing built-up areas of the Corridor must become more dense. The single-family detached home has been the essential building block of the Arizona lifestyle. Higher-density developments, ranging from patio homes with community swimming pools to multilevel condominiums, consume less water on a per capita basis. Smaller lots present less landscaping area and have a proportionally greater area covered by impervious surfaces like roofs and driveways. At significantly higher population densities, in multi-family apartments or condominiums, landscaping per resident is even further reduced and may be subject to professional management. Work by Professor Patricia Gober at Arizona State University (ASU) suggests a dramatic decline in per capita water use at increasing density.[21] But her colleague Ray Quay cautions that recent Phoenix data suggest a need to revisit this relationship. Density may not always be the critical variable; income can be as significant at higher densities as it is in single-family developments.

The Lifestyle of Affluence. Low-density single-family homes, lush landscaping, golf courses, and multiple cars are all part of the lifestyle of affluent twentieth-century Americans. In the hot desert of central Arizona, there is another simple proxy for that lifestyle: about 40 percent of metropolitan Phoenix residents have private backyard pools, one of the highest percentages in the world.[22] Many consider their pools essential

Figures 2.6a and 2.6b. A view of two multi-family projects. Though the one on the top is higher density, its lush landscaping results in relatively high per capita water use. On the bottom, a lower-density project may actually require less water per capita. (Sources: 2.6a, Photo by author; 2.6b, Photo courtesy of Community of Civano, LLC)

to a bearable summer. The average backyard pool holds about 16,000 gallons of water.[23] Evaporation and backwashing result in the loss of around 20,000 gallons or more per pool each year.[24] Further, most pool maintenance companies recommend that each pool be fully drained and refilled every few years solely for the purpose of keeping the appropriate chemical balance.

Private swimming pools are an icon of a lifestyle of abundance that may be coming to a close for a variety of reasons related to average income, the price of housing, the size of lots, and a host of deep changes in the nature of society. Indeed, recent evidence indicates that the percentage of newly constructed homes with swimming pools is plummeting—by one estimate, down to as low as 10 percent.[25] This particular use of relatively cheap, apparently abundant water also crystallizes a sense of choices and priorities about living in the Sun Corridor. Will the day come when pool construction is limited to pools serving larger numbers of people? Or is it more important to continue allowing individual pools? Is this an issue to be resolved through regulation, or by price, or through evolving social preferences? Should residents be willing to give up the right to a backyard pool in order to guarantee a more reliable water supply, to maintain local agriculture, to support natural ecosystems, or to allow more people to move into the Sun Corridor?

Landscaping. If Phoenix were to stop watering its existing Midwestern plant palette, the grass and trees would die and the area would become markedly more barren. Some of the trees that would die are fifty years old and more. Some are located on old golf courses, in historic neighborhoods with an agricultural heritage, in city parks, or on the ASU campus. Should some of this landscape go? Phoenix will only reach Tucson's per capita consumption range through such drastic action. Doing so would be at odds with Phoenix's history—and may exacerbate the "heat island" effect. But reducing water use for landscaping remains the most effective way to stretch the water supply. Should Phoenix give up the "oasis" nature of the older parts of the city in order to accommodate even more residents?

A major trend is appearing in Phoenix: the use of artificial turf in residential landscapes. In southern Nevada, water authorities have paid out about $200 million to incentivize the removal of real grass turf. Some Arizona cities have followed suit. But consumers are choosing to remove grass and replace it with artificial turf (at a cost of about $10 per square foot) in order to save water and avoid mowing, and—most often cited reason—"because the dogs really like it."[26]

Aesthetics and Urban Environment. On July 20, 2010, the rubberized dam that held back the Tempe Town Lake cracked and burst. Hundreds of millions of gallons of water moving at 15,000 cubic feet per second rushed down the Salt River channel.[27] Following the break, some people called for not refilling the lake because it was a "waste of water." Tempe, however, cites the lake as the second-most-visited tourist attraction in Arizona (after the Grand Canyon). The city also views the lake as an engine of economic development because apartments, condominiums, offices, and other development have occurred along its shores. Perhaps most importantly, the lake has become a gathering place in an urban area that too often seems merely a seamless web of beige houses and big-box retail centers. If metro Phoenix is to offer the kind of urban excitement and amenities other cities have, it will require "punctuation marks" throughout the urban fabric that concentrate populations and convene people for social and cultural reasons. Harbors, rivers, and lakes have always been places where people congregate.

Is this an appropriate use of water? While the use is controversial, it is, after all, putting water back into a riverbed—is that

Figures 2.7a and 2.7b. The home on the top is typical of a Phoenix subdivision. The home below is in the more-arid landscape of Civano, a Tucson master-planned community. (Sources: 2.7a, Art Holeman Photography; 2.7b, Arizona State University, Morrison Institute, Watering the Sun Corridor)

Figure 2.8. Buildings along the Salt River Project canal in Scottsdale's waterfront district. (© Shutterstock: Chris Curtis)

really a bad thing? Similar uses exist in Scottsdale's Indian Bend Wash. In Phoenix, the Rio Salado restoration area has been reconstructed for bird and animal habitat as well as hiking. These are examples of how water can be used to focus development and activity to create a more urban place. A less water-consumptive alternative to Tempe Town Lake might have been possible, but using water to celebrate life in an arid environment is basic to a shared civilization. Even in an arid place, cities can and should integrate water into the urban environment in a way that is both efficient and also provides amenities and supports natural systems. Canals run throughout many urban areas and can serve as paths and trails. Historically, many canals were lined with trees that were cut down to save water—only to use that water to plant new trees in individual backyards. Cutting off uses of water for its life-giving quality in the desert simply to support more residents does not seem to be a clearly rational choice.

While there has been much discussion over the years about the potential of Phoenix canals as urban amenities, it is only recently that some actual change has begun.[28] For decades, the canal banks served as informal walking and jogging paths, but the Salt River Project resisted physical improvement of the banks because of maintenance needs. SRP itself began to celebrate canals with a public art project called Arizona Falls and then cooperated with the City of Scottsdale to create the Scottsdale Waterfront—a center for high-density residential, office, and restaurant activity along the canal.

The Natural Environment. The most fundamental trade-off of all is the question of determining to what extent the natural environment of ephemeral desert washes, free-flowing streams, and riparian habitats deserves to be protected. In the era of Manifest Destiny and the settling of the West, the answer seemed obvious: uses for people, in farming and building settlements, trumped all natural things. Dams, canals, pumps, irrigation, and long-distance conveyance of water all evince that decision. In central Arizona, there is not much natural use of water left. The pressures to continue building a huge urban area in the desert will increasingly require dewatering an ever-larger area. It is often said that the era of dam and great canal building is over, partly because many of the best sites are already used, partly because of today's environmental demands, and partly because America's appetite for building great public works seems diminished. But to what extent should protection or even restoration of the natural environment be a high priority in water-use choices?

An important consideration here is that at this juncture the environmental costs are not merely incremental. Loss of remaining riparian or wetland habitat has huge ramifications. In the arid West, rivers, streams, and wetlands are where wildlife concentrates, especially migrating wildlife. Something like 85 percent of Sonoran species depend on rivers at some point in their life

Figure 2.9. The Tempe Town Lake returned water to the historic bed of the Salt River. Downtown Phoenix is in the distant background. (© Shutterstock: Tim Roberts Photography)

cycles. In the last century, human interventions have rendered a significant amount of riparian and wetland habitat nonfunctional or even nonexistent.

All of the issues discussed above represent the crux of a debate about water use in the West that must unfold over the next decades. The future involves complex societal choices that will necessarily be made through a combination of market forces, government regulations, and behavioral attitudes.

One of the thorniest dilemmas of water use is price. Historically, Americans have had an attitude that water should be a public-use good almost like air—largely free for the taking. Municipal water rates are a complex equation, based largely on the cost of delivery, and often include other utility services like wastewater disposal and trash collection. As a result, price signals about water use are often obscured. Water is still cheap even in the desert Southwest. Table 2.2 shows the comparative rankings of monthly water bills for some of the largest cities in the United States. Phoenix ranks relatively low, and even at the highest levels of usage, it ranks only in the middle. Tucson, by contrast, has a rate structure using aggressive block pricing—the more you use, the more expensive it gets. Such a structure would encourage more conservation in Phoenix. It would also mean that much of the historic landscape of Phoenix would be abandoned as too expensive. Water conservation would come at the cost of a drier, hotter, and less attractive environment. That future may be unavoidable, but so far the city has largely resisted a debate over dramatically altering pricing policies.[29]

Table 2.2. Typical Monthly Water Bills among the Fifty Largest US Cities Ranked from lowest (1) to highest (50).

	3,750 Gallons	7,500 Gallons	15,000 Gallons
Phoenix	3	2	19
Tucson	17	15	37
Albuquerque	28	20	8
Atlanta	42	47	49
Chicago	7	6	9
Denver	15	17	20
Las Vegas	32	21	12
Los Angeles	24	35	39
Seattle	49	50	50

Source: Black and Veatch Water Rate Survey, 2012–13 Report.

While water management is *the* great lesson of what Phoenix has done well, sustaining urbanism in central Arizona requires continued creative thinking, complex balancing between competing uses, and the kind of committed collective decision making that was a hallmark of bringing civilization to the desert.

Chapter 3

Coping with Heat

Cᴌɪᴍᴀᴛᴇ ᴄʜᴀɴɢᴇ ᴜsᴇᴅ ᴛᴏ ʙᴇ ᴄᴀʟʟᴇᴅ "global warming." Both
terms are still around, but the use of *climate change* has become far
more prevalent. *Global warming* was a way to refer to the overall
rise in average temperatures as a result of the greenhouse effect—
man-made carbon dioxide spewed into the atmosphere, resulting
in trapping more solar energy and heating up the planet. *Climate
change* has a couple of advantages as a moniker. First, it conveys
the possibility that it is not just warming to worry about, but also
increases in things like hurricanes, tornadoes, and heavy precipitation caused by atmospheric changes. Second, it provides a simpler
way of asserting: "I don't know if it's caused by humans or not,
but clearly things are changing and we need to react." Many scientists and commentators continue to use the terms interchange-
ably, sometimes choosing the term that will seem more (or less)

threatening to the intended audience. If you want to worry people in Phoenix, *global warming* is your semantic choice.

Phoenix is inarguably one of the world's hottest cities, depending on how *hot* is defined. Tropical cities have higher average mean temperatures, since there is less variation between summer and winter. By that measure, Miami (average mean of 77°F) beats Phoenix (average mean of 75°F). But Phoenix exceeds at the extremes, with an average daily high temperature of 87.2°F, highest in the United States, and Phoenix has by far the most days with a high temperature over 99°F, at 107 (Las Vegas is a distant second at 70 days).[1] For average daily high temperatures in July, Phoenix, at 107°F, is exceeded only by a few cities in the Middle East, such as Ahvaz, Iran, and Kuwait City, each at 115°F.[2] And Phoenix is getting hotter. Since 1990, Phoenix has set 144 record daytime highs and 230 record nighttime highs.

Jerry Adler, writing in *Smithsonian* in May 2014, painted a bleak picture of the future Phoenix. He examines the link between high temperatures and anger, noting that expressions like "hotheads" or "fired up" are based on social dysfunction flowing from being too hot. Empirical evidence suggests that crime rates rise with higher temperature (though maybe that's just idle youth in the summer). "Science fiction is one way to get a feel for what daily life might be like in a hotter world," Adler writes. "Another way is to go to Phoenix during a late-September heat wave when temperatures hover around 105°F, where the first thing you learn about the future is that it will apparently be lived indoors."[3]

Since the earliest days of settlement, Phoenicians have sought a way to insulate themselves from the summer's heat.[4] Ironically, continuing to use the indigenous construction of thick-walled, small-windowed adobe buildings would have provided some help, but such buildings were rejected by the early white settlers as "uncivilized." Sleeping porches were a partial response to the climate, since the dry desert cooled down at night. On those porches, citizens might find the only way to go to sleep was by wrapping themselves in wet sheets before lying down on a bed or cot, or by hanging the wet sheets up around the edge of the porch, creating a primitive form of evaporative cooling.[5]

Combining the wet sheet with an electric fan created the earliest successful mechanical device for home cooling. An evaporative cooler lowered air temperature by injecting water into it, raising the humidity. However, this method works only when the humidity is very low. This meant it was not useful for cooling most of the southern United States, and worked in Phoenix only until the late-summer monsoon caused the humidity to rise above 15 or 20 percent.

What is today recognized as an air conditioner—a machine that cools the air while dehumidifying—was essentially invented in 1902 by Willis Carrier.[6] Most of the early applications of air-conditioning were for major industrial buildings, since the machines were huge, expensive, and dangerous (the coolant was a toxic ammonia compound). As refrigerant chemicals were improved and as the units became more manageable in size, air conditioners moved into office buildings. Air-conditioning began to penetrate the American consciousness when it started arriving in movie theaters in the early 1920s.

The first widespread application of air-conditioning to houses were window units, which first appeared after World War II. Sales jumped from 75,000 in 1948 to more than a million by 1953. According to Newsweek's Malcolm Jones Jr., "The dripping box jutting out of the bedroom window joined the TV aerial on the roof as instant fixtures in the American suburban landscape."[7] By the end of the 1940s, Phoenix led the nation in the number of home air-conditioning units installed. Promoters who in the past had gone out of their way to avoid mentioning hot summers now explained that air-conditioning made Phoenix just like anywhere else in the country.

Central home air-conditioning gained acceptance more slowly, in part due to cost. Initially, the Federal Housing Administration (FHA) was unwilling to factor central air into its mortgages. When

Figure 3.1. Train car delivery of home air-conditioning units. (Source: John F. Long)

the agency reversed itself in 1957, installation boomed.[8] By 1960, the census reported that in Phoenix more households had central air than window units—nearly 25 percent of all houses.

In the early 1950s, a Motorola executive named Dan Noble began moving electronics manufacturing to Phoenix. In order to maintain a constant temperature and dust-free environment, Motorola's facilities were all air-conditioned. Besides setting the city on a high-tech trajectory, his decision spurred the rapid rise of air-conditioning: "Refrigeration cooling has transformed Phoenix into a year-round city of delightful living."[9] Motorola's engineers got used to their air-conditioned factories and saw no reason why their houses should not be just as comfortable.

Air-conditioning had an enormous social impact on the development of postwar America. The rise of the Sunbelt as the center for American growth in the 1960s coincides with market penetration by central air-conditioning. Air-conditioning enabled people living in Houston or Atlanta or Phoenix to dress like people in New York or Chicago and to shop for the same kinds of soft goods. The physical appearance of communities also changed to adapt to the new technology. The demise of neighborhood sociability represented in the loss of the front porch is often blamed on the automobile. Air-conditioning and television probably had far more impact on where Americans chose to spend their time when they were at home. No longer was it necessary to sit outside in the evening to cool off. Inside was both comfort and entertainment.

Air-conditioning finally allowed Phoenix to become the American metropolis it had long aspired to be. During the 1950s, the city's population increased by 311 percent, the highest rate of growth among the nation's fifty largest cities. In 1959, there was more construction in Phoenix than in all the years from 1914 to 1946. By 1960, it was the largest city in the Southwest, with a population of 439,000.

Despite the widespread acceptance of air-conditioning—and its extraordinary market penetration today (87 percent of American homes have some form of air-conditioning[10])—there is sometimes a tendency to view air-conditioning as a wasteful frill. Heating, on the other hand, has been around for millennia and is simply a necessity of life. Kate Murphy's 2015 diatribe against air-conditioning, appearing in the *New York Times*, is typical:

> Why is America so over air-conditioned? It seems absurd, if not unconscionable, when you consider the money and energy wasted—not to mention the negative impact on the environment from the associated greenhouse-gas emissions. Architects, engineers, building owners, and energy experts sigh with exasperation when asked for an explanation. They tick off a number of reasons—probably the most vexing is cultural.
>
> "Being able to make people feel cold in the summer is a sign of power and prestige," said Richard de Dear, director

of the Indoor Environmental Quality Laboratory at the University of Sydney, Australia, where excessive air-conditioning is as prevalent as it is in much of the United States.[11]

Slate columnist Daniel Engber has taken on the defense of air-conditioning as something of a *cause célèbre*. In two columns in 2012, he analyzed the American policy bias against air-conditioning. Federal subsidies have long been far more plentiful for heating than for cooling. A series of critiques of the rise in air-conditioning use seem to assume it is a negative, even though the nationwide southward migration has produced a net decline in energy use for climate control.[12] In 2015, Engber offered this response to Kate Murphy's piece:

> Anti-AC sentiment persists in spite of basic facts, and without convincing evidence. It relies instead on naked ideology and posture. To rail against the air conditioner is a way for cosmopolitans to claim their bona fides, and to place themselves in opposition to irresponsible American excess. When they proudly say they'd rather use electric fans, they show their neighbors that they're tasteful intellectuals— right-minded and upstanding. That is to say, they're members of the brrr-geoisie.[13]

NYU professor Andrew Needham's 2015 book, *Power Lines*, posits that the coal mines of the Black Mesa on the Navajo Reservation in northeastern Arizona were a direct result of the profligate and wasteful energy needs of Phoenix. He offers this thesis without ever examining how much energy Phoenix uses compared to other places. Rory Carroll, writing in the *Guardian*, notes that the United States consumes more energy for air-conditioning than the rest of the world combined, and more energy for cooling than the continent of Africa uses for all purposes. This balance will shift, as the proportion of Chinese homes with air-conditioning rocketed from 8 percent to 70 percent between 1995 and 2004.[14]

A rise in the use of air-conditioning in China represents a net new energy use. People moving from cold climates to warmer ones in the United States, however, do not necessarily have the same impact. The reality is that by most comparative measures, metropolitan Phoenix is less impactful in its energy consumption than many other American cities. The US Department of Energy puts the average national per capita residential energy consumption at $3,052 per year. Arizona comes in at $2,628, 15 percent below the US average, ranking forty-seventh among the states.[15]

In a March 2013 environmental research letter, Michael Sivak of the University of Michigan Transportation Research Institute cites his study showing the favorable side of cooling over heating in terms of energy consumption: "The results indicate that climate control in Minneapolis is about 3.5 times as energy demanding as in Miami. This finding suggests that, in the US, living in cold climates is more energy demanding than living in hot climates."[16]

Viewed in terms of carbon footprint, this energy consumption statistic becomes even more positive (see table 3.1). Much of Phoenix's electricity is generated by nuclear power. And while a fair amount is generated by coal, those large coal-fired generating stations do have scrubbers, making them less polluting than the diesel oil–fueled furnaces used for heating homes in the Midwest. Analysis done by the Center for Climate Strategies indicates that Arizona emits on average 14 metric tons of CO_2e (carbon dioxide equivalent) per person, while the US average is closer to 22 metric tons.[17] The difference is the result of warmer temperature, the lack of heavy industry, newer and more efficient building stock, and a generally newer fleet of automobiles.

Predictions for climate change indicate a high degree of likelihood that Phoenix and other Western cities will get still hotter. The reality is that a given city or even an urban region can do very little about staving off the impact of changes in the global climate. The

Table 3.1. Per Capita Carbon Emissions from Residential Energy Use, 2005

Metropolitan Statistical Areas	Metric Tons
Washington–Arlington–Alexandria (DC-VA-MD-WV) MSA	1.958
Dallas–Fort Worth–Arlington (TX) MSA	1.177
Philadelphia–Camden–Wilmington (PA-NJ-DE-MD) MSA	1.114
Atlanta–Sandy Springs–Marietta (GA) MSA	1.049
Salt Lake City (UT) MSA	1.046
Denver–Aurora–Bloomfield (CO) MSA	1.025
Detroit–Warren–Livonia (MI) MSA	1.002
Boston–Cambridge–Quincy (MA-NH) MSA	0.996
Tampa–St. Petersburg–Clearwater (FL) MSA	0.988
Houston–Sugar Land–Baytown (TX) MSA	0.983
Las Vegas–Paradise (NV) MSA	0.981
Miami–Fort Lauderdale–Miami Beach (FL)	0.861
Chicago–Joliet–Naperville (IL-IN-WI) MSA	0.833
Charlotte–Gastonia–Rock Hill (NC-SC) MSA	0.792
New York–Northern New Jersey–Long Island (NY-NJ-PA) MSA	0.670
Phoenix–Mesa–Glendale (AZ) MSA	0.658
Los Angeles–Long Beach–Santa Ana (CA) MSA	0.391
San Francisco–Oakland–Fremont (CA) MSA	0.390
San Jose–Sunnyvale–Santa Clara (CA) MSA	0.389
Riverside–San Bernardino–Ontario (CA) MSA	0.372
San Diego–Carlsbad–San Marcos (CA) MSA	0.360
Seattle–Tacoma–Bellevue (WA) MSA	0.356

Source: Brookings Institution, *Shrinking the Carbon Footprint of America*, 2008.

goal of a given region, therefore, must be to find ways to adapt and survive in the face of a changing climate.

Obviously, for Arizona the first solution is again technology. Air-conditioning made it possible to live in a place as fiercely hot as the Sonoran Desert. As temperature has risen over the last few decades, air-conditioning has continued to keep the place comfortable enough that it still attracts major in-migration. Even with a significant temperature rise, it is likely that air-conditioning can continue to make the interiors of buildings and cars relatively comfortable. This is an area where technology has evolved rapidly over time and become more energy-efficient, and it is likely to continue to do so. Solar energy holds particular promise for continuing to air-condition a sunny place.

All the sunshine that makes it hot in Phoenix obviously has a corollary benefit. Solar energy is increasingly poised to be one of the long-term potential solutions to the end of the era of cheap, petroleum-based energy. Arizona was an early pioneer in solar energy research, hosting an international conference in the late 1950s. In 2008, then-Governor Janet Napolitano said that Arizona had the potential to be "the Persian Gulf of Solar Energy."[18] Under Napolitano's administration, Arizona developed a robust suite of incentives and a generous "net metering" policy. Both utility-scale and rooftop solar installations began to soar. In 2014, the state ranked fourth for total installations—behind California, North Carolina, Nevada, and Massachusetts.[19]

Phoenix's suburban fabric of single-family homes and sun-baked roofs is especially well suited to individual rooftop panels. By 2014, statewide residential installations were estimated at 35,000 houses, with the vast majority in Maricopa County. The solar industry is still emergent, however, and has been heavily dependent on subsidies and incentives. Arizona has a traditional reluctance to use the power of government to encourage economic change. The Arizona Corporation Commission (ACC), the state regulatory body over utility companies, began in 2013 to roll back virtually all commercial incentives and restrict residential benefits.[20]

The solar energy equation is complex because solar power is intermittent and relatively unpredictable, even in a place as sunny as Arizona. It is difficult to use distributed (rooftop-based), intermittent solar power as a means of obviating the need for a full, robust generation system and grid. To utility companies, distributed solar power can seem like an existential threat: it results in electricity they cannot control, which they are sometimes mandated to purchase from

Figure 3.2. Solar panels in the desert. (© Shutterstock: Andrei Orlov)

individual consumers even though they may not need it, and they must provide a full backup in the case of the failure of solar energy-generating systems. This complex balancing act has led to vicious fights over the extent to which other utility customers should be subsidizing those who have solar units on their houses. The solution typically proposed by utility companies is for a fixed monthly fee to be paid by any customer with solar generating capacity.

In 2014, the complexity of the utility-customer solar equation in Arizona erupted into open warfare. Arizona Public Service (APS), the state's and Phoenix's largest utility, went on the offensive, seeking from the ACC the right to impose a $50 monthly charge for "grid access" by solar homes. The ACC ultimately approved one-tenth of that request—a $5 monthly charge. Thereafter, the next election for ACC members, historically an obscure office, became hotly and expensively contested. The assumption was that APS made huge contributions to pro-utility candidates, who were ultimately elected.[21]

In December 2014, Arizona's second-largest electricity provider, the Salt River Project (SRP), imposed a $50 monthly "grid access" charge on its customers.[22] As a public entity, SRP is not regulated by the ACC.

The combination of diminished incentives, grid access charges, and ongoing controversy has resulted in slowing rooftop installations and in some installation companies dramatically reducing their workforce. But continuing efficiency improvements and falling prices mean that solar will continue to gain market share, albeit more slowly.

Ultimately, another technological leap is needed to make solar energy more reliable. That could come in the form of sophisticated batteries that would store solar energy for future distribution. There have been suggestions that solar energy should be used to power pumped-storage units that raise water which can subsequently be dropped through turbines for generation. One major proposed solar power generating station in Arizona would create a giant greenhouse with a chimney in the middle. The air that is warmed within the greenhouse would then result in an updraft through the chimney. Near the outer edge of the greenhouse the updraft would cause a series of wind turbines to turn, generating power. This system could operate for a much longer period of time during the day and on cloudy days, thus giving solar power generation a more reliable profile.

Whatever happens with solar generation in the future, Arizona is likely to be one of the principal beneficiaries of this cleaner power-generating system. Much of that power will undoubtedly be used to mitigate the heat that makes it hard to live in the desert.

There are, however, local climate phenomena whereby local actions can make a major difference in future livability.

An overall rise in temperature, and particularly the rise in night-time low temperatures, threatens a place like Phoenix where outdoor living is a critical part of the lifestyle. As the portion of the year in which temperatures exceed 100°F increases and as the nighttime low temperatures creep ever upward, enjoying an outdoor sporting event, allowing kids to play outdoors, or even going for a walk or bicycle ride becomes increasingly uncomfortable. This is a very real problem, which at some point could result in more and more people deciding that they no longer want to live in so hot a place.

One particular consequence of urbanizing in hot locations that is especially challenging for Phoenix is known as the urban heat island. It is well documented that urban areas result in raising the ambient temperature of their geography. The reasons include a shift in land cover from plant materials to pavement, concrete, and buildings, as well as the generation of waste heat from air-conditioning units, emissions from factories, and the use of automobiles. Scientists at ASU found that increases in the urban heat island intensity in urban Phoenix coincided with increased total peak energy demand for residential and commercial cooling between 1950 and 2000.[23] Energy demands increased because of more residents using air-conditioning units for longer periods of time.[24]

In Phoenix, the urban heat island has tended to dramatically raise the nighttime low temperature: the city no longer cools off on summer nights as it did when it was smaller. Most of the evidence indicates that the urban heat island is a "plateau" of elevating temperatures over what would have been natural nighttime low temperatures. Additional urbanization does not appear to further raise the effect of the heat island but rather simply to spread it out farther as the city grows.[25]

Greater Phoenix is getting hotter and staying hotter for longer periods of time. Since 1949, the average low temperature at Sky Harbor International Airport has risen by more than ten degrees Fahrenheit. The Phoenix urban heat island case study shows a strong departure from normal variability beginning in the mid-1960s, when the mean minimum temperature began to rise sharply from 72°F in the 1990–94 period to 75°F in the 2000–2004 timeframe.

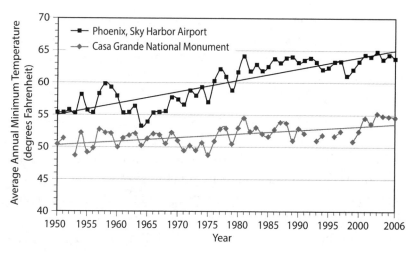

Figure 3.3. The urban heat island effect raises daily low temperatures. (Source: Zack Guido, "Urban Heat Island: Raising City Temperatures," CLIMAS, University of Arizona, http://www.southwestclimatechange.org/impacts/people/urban-heat-island, accessed October 5, 2015)

This was especially pronounced in the urban fringe, where suburbanization was replacing desert landscapes and farming areas.

This phenomenon is not unique to Phoenix. The heat island effect has been measured in urban areas around the world. During the day in undeveloped landscapes, solar energy is absorbed by plants and is dissipated in the vegetation and soil. This results in the cooling effect that compensates for some increases in temperature. In cities, the built environment absorbs solar energy, warms the surrounding air, and radiates it back at night. The agricultural areas around Phoenix actually enjoyed more of a cooling effect at night than did the desert because of water evaporation. The densely urbanized areas of Phoenix show the least natural cooling, but there are pockets of cool temperatures throughout metropolitan Phoenix, such as the Arcadia area where the preserved orchard trees, expansive grassy lots, and "flood irrigation" watering systems result in higher humidity and less heat given off at night.

The change from the shrubbery, grass, and green tree landscaping of Phoenix toward decomposed granite, cactus, and desert plants in order to conserve water may, in some instances, exacerbate the heat island effect. This is a complex relationship that has not yet been well studied. The decline in agriculture will also exacerbate the heat island effect became planted fields actually cool off at night even more than did the raw desert.

Dense urban canyons (walls of tall buildings lining both sides of a street) increase the total urban surface area for energy storage radiation and reduce urban wind speed, and therefore tend to raise the ambient low temperatures of an area. This may suggest that a more carefully dispersed pattern of taller buildings with greater setbacks is appropriate in warmer climates. This runs counter to the instinct of planners and city officials to want more intense urban uses pushed close to the street so as to create intense activity nodes.

Other states, cities, and countries have initiated programs to deal with the urban heat island effect. California has a cool-roof rebate to provide an incentive for construction projects providing reflective roofing. Los Angeles has aggressively removed paved schoolyards and replaced them with green open space. Salt Lake City, Sacramento, and Davis have all established parking-lot paving regulations. Phoenix is experimenting with cooler pavement—colored and perhaps permeable.[26]

Melbourne, Australia, may be at the forefront of efforts to deal with urban heat island effects. After a 2009 heat wave that peaked at 113°F (a nearly "routine" summer high in Phoenix) sparked power outages and culminated in wildfires, the city launched an ambitious initiative seeking to lower its average temperature by seven degrees.[27] Melbourne's plan to mitigate the heat island is to plant 30,000 trees in the central business area, thus creating the kind of "garden city" once dreamed about by urban visionaries. Melbourne, like Phoenix, has to balance the need to minimize water use with the need to plant a tree canopy that can cool the city. In Melbourne, a vast scheme to capture storm-water runoff and store it for watering local trees was part of the solution.

A few cities in central Arizona have begun to encourage or even incentivize the removal of grass and its replacement with desert landscaping or artificial turf. Removing grass in a hot city and replacing it with crushed granite and cactus may have the negative impact of increasing the heat island effect. The environmental impact of artificial turf is not well documented, but certainly artificial turf is cooler than granite. Negative effects from the loss of grass can be mitigated by careful introduction of appropriate drought-tolerant trees. In Arizona, that means palo verde, palo brea, mesquite, and other native and nonnative arid-region species.

In addition to using trees to mitigate the heat island, it will also be critical in an age of ever-higher temperatures to use trees and built structures to provide shade on sidewalks, paths, and areas where people congregate. In Phoenix, the use of stretched shade fabric on school playgrounds, public plazas, and sporting venues has increased dramatically in the last twenty years. These "umbrellas" are a direct response to increasing temperatures and the need for providing more shade.

High-pressure water misting systems are even used in shopping areas and outdoor restaurants to introduce the evaporative cooling effect and create small microclimates. While this use of water mist is often criticized by visitors to the metropolitan Phoenix area, it is in fact a response to local climate concerns little different from outdoor patio heaters in colder climates. These kinds of small targeted efforts to create microclimates are a rational response to increasing temperatures.

High temperatures and aridity have another serious consequence for livability and public health: air quality.

Phoenix undeniably has an air-quality problem. Even if there were no cars, the combination of dust, sunshine, and farming would create challenges. The US EPA ranks Maricopa County seventh in the number of unhealthy days for lung diseases behind Salt Lake

City, Detroit, Philadelphia, Chicago, Houston, and not surprisingly, Los Angeles, which is way out in front on this scale.

Nevertheless, with regard to air quality Phoenix has been very successful in many measures of reduction. In 1984, Maricopa County had seventy-six days in one year in which it exceeded the carbon monoxide standards. There have been no days in violation of the standard since the year 2000. In the 1970s, the lead standards were exceeded about eighty days a year. There have been no days exceeding lead standards since 1988, due to the policy of removing lead from gasoline.

Ozone remains an problem, where Maricopa County remains a marginal non-attainment area exceeding the standards approximately twenty-seven days each year. Much of this is because of the interaction between volatile organic compounds and sunlight. It is with regard to particulates that Maricopa County has its greatest air-quality challenges. The PM 2.5 standard, which is essentially smoke and soot, is frequently exceeded in the winter when air inversions hold down the emissions from wood-burning fireplaces. As a result, Maricopa County has banned wood-burning fireplaces in new residential construction and issues no-burn-day pronouncements on most holidays. The PM 10 standard, which covers dust, is the most problematic metric: Maricopa County never reached attainment until 2014. This is likely to remain a difficult problem to solve. Maricopa County has made great strides, though, in decreasing dust from construction sites. One of the most sweeping solutions, which has been proposed at various times, is to increase the amount of pavement of roads, alleys, and parking lots in the fringes of the city. Doing so will decrease dust, but likely increase the heat island effect.

The desert is a dusty place, particularly when wind whips up dust on farms south of town, creating the dramatic and spectacular haboobs. The natural Sonoran Desert was not usually a place of great sandstorms. Rather, it formed a relatively hard crust that was broken up by cactus and creosote bushes. But

Figure 3.4. The haboob rolling into Phoenix. (Source: Flickr, Alan Stark)

farming bladed and tilled that land, exposing loose particles and putting more dust into the air. In a desert thunderstorm, as the storm collapses, a sudden downdraft will set in motion an immense cloud of loose sand or dust, stirring up a ground-level dust cloud. These huge, slow-moving walls of dust get national coverage because they are so spectacular, creating the impression of a cataclysmic weather event like a tornado. While it is unpleasant to be outside in a haboob, and while haboobs may contribute to additional non-attainment days, for most Phoenicians, the main consequence of a desert haboob is a dirty swimming pool. As houses replace more farms, one consequence will likely be fewer dust storms.

It is possible that air quality may limit the growth of cities like Phoenix. The federal government's 2015 Clean Power Plan creates major challenges for newer Western cities. For a place like Phoenix, the ozone, carbon dioxide, and particulate standards driven by greenhouse-gas concerns create a particular dilemma. Because Phoenix has little heavy industry and no coal-fired generating plants immediately nearby, its percentage target is much more difficult to reach than a place having older, dirtier polluters. In fact, Arizona starts with pollution levels that are lower than the end goal of some states. Initially, the plan called for Arizona to achieve a 52 percent reduction—an extremely challenging number given an already cleaner set of power plants than in Eastern states. As a result of extensive efforts by the state's Department of Environmental Quality, the reduction was changed to 34 percent, with a slower phase-in.[28] The goals now seem achievable.

Bill deBuys has explained that in Europe, heat waves in the high nineties often kill hundreds of people. Phoenix, he asserts, is likely headed toward a similar future.[29] His *Los Angeles Times* article appeared in March 2013. The previous year, Phoenix experienced fourteen days over 110°F. The city recorded twenty-one heat-caused and twenty-two heat-related deaths, a tragic number—virtually all related to an absence of air-conditioning. But as *USA Today* pointed out in 2015, cold weather is twenty times as deadly as hot weather in the United States.[30]

Heat and poor air quality also pose serious threats to the third circle of the sustainability trinity: social equity. Heat and respiratory deaths are unevenly distributed to lower-income areas where people cannot afford air-conditioning or may turn off their units due to utility costs. There tends to be less shade—fewer trees—in lower-income areas. Most of those who die from heat tend to be homeless—with nowhere to live and an inability to migrate to cooler places in the summer. If climate change and the heat island combine to drive nighttime lows seven to ten degrees higher, the social costs will be significant.

Harvey Bryan, an architecture professor at ASU, points out that much of this negative impact can be mitigated by less paving, more trees, narrower streets, broader overhangs, thicker walls, better insulation, lighter paint colors, and a variety of relatively low-tech interventions in urban design.

Higher-technology solutions are also a major part of the solution. The new cities of the arid West were built with great reliance on the technologies of hydrology, air-conditioning, and transportation. These technologies made it possible for the "carrying capacity" of challenging geographies to be greatly increased. It is this history that gives rise to much of the criticism that these places are presumptively unsustainable. But their historical ability to meet challenges with technological solutions may actually create greater capacity to confront increasing future demands.

Throughout history, technology has provided a way of taking what seems to be an insoluble problem and turning it into a price problem. The Industrial Revolution was made possible first by coal and subsequently by oil, both of which served to replace human and animal power with a more efficient and cost-effective source of energy. The uninhabitable aridity of the American West was solved by massive, and highly subsidized, water systems that made it possible to create a reliable water supply in places with very little rainfall. More recently, the overreliance of the United States on foreign oil with its energy and national security risks has, at least for the time being, been solved by the use of hydraulic fracturing ("fracking") technology to make available American-produced oil and natural gas.

It is overly simplistic to assume that technology can always provide a solution—but this has, indeed, been much of the history of urban growth. Air-conditioning made it possible to live in a place that was otherwise simply too hot. So while it is too facile to assert that technology will take care of whatever problems of sustainability arise in the future, it is also far too apocalyptic to assume that whatever looks like an insoluble problem today will remain insoluble tomorrow.

In fact, Phoenix is an example of a city already positioned to deal with climate change. It was built in a place that was climatically challenged from the outset—one of the hottest and driest places on the planet. For a place like Phoenix, the challenges of climate change are most likely to be increases in the challenges it has always faced: it is likely to get hotter and drier. Ultimately, Sunbelt cities may be less vulnerable than older cities that were built with an expectation of a less extreme climate.

Chapter 4

Transportation and the Suburban City

 T HE AUTOMOBILE IS THE CENTRAL villain in any story about the suburbs, sprawl, and the ills of the contemporary city. Some of this blame may be unfair, but the automobile was the most dramatic and significant change in the way people lived during the twentieth century. It was the automobile that made it possible for a vast swath of society to live in single-family detached homes but nevertheless reach their jobs efficiently. It was the automobile that permitted places of work to scatter about the landscape rather than being concentrated within walking distance of one another. It was the automobile that resulted in acres and acres of urban areas being given over to asphalt, both in ever-wider streets and in parking lots. It was the automobile that caused buildings to be set back from the street and separated from one another. And of course, it was the automobile that begat smog and contributed so greatly to climate change. So through the rich literature of modern urban criticism, the city without the automobile has become the Holy Grail. The urban form of the automobile-dependent city poses challenges not just for the Sunbelt but also for cities throughout the United States and around the world.

It is easy to see how a high-density city like New York can survive without private cars. Indeed, most people who live in Manhattan do exactly that. Imagining how the auto-dependent urban form evolves into the future often leads people to try to figure out how to convert places like Phoenix into places more like Manhattan. A bit of this thinking is occasionally a useful exercise, but it is unreasonable to think that the entire urban fabric of a city of a thousand or more square miles with more than a million single-family detached houses should be completely transformed into an utterly different kind of place. The challenge, rather, is to think about how the urban form of the suburban city can remain functional, accessible, and desirable in a different time with changing modes of transport. Phoenix's history with transportation alternatives is instructive.

Private automobiles arrived in Phoenix around the summer of 1900 and were an instant hit.[1] Hard, flat ground meant that cars were useful even without paved roads. By 1910, there were 382 licensed cars in Phoenix, and an automobile club was lobbying for roads to other Arizona cities. A special municipal committee visited Los Angeles, El Paso, and other cities to study street pavement. Based on their recommendations, nineteen blocks of the business core were paved. In 1920, a local official said, "The people in this town have forgotten how to walk. If they have to go two blocks, they get in a machine and drive."[2] Reflecting this growing attachment to motor travel, the number of cars registered in Maricopa County rose from 646 in 1913 to 11,539 in 1920, and to 53,064 in 1929.[3]

Streetcars had allowed cities to spread out along linear spokes, and filling in between the spokes was limited by how far residents could comfortably walk. Cars broke this pattern. As a result, new real estate was opened up for development, and the city form changed from a hub with spokes to an ever-expanding grid of blocks linked by asphalt. New subdivisions served only by the automobile were beginning to dominate the growth pattern of most Western cities by the 1920s.[4]

The auto did not just represent an easier way to get around—it was heralded as a transformative yet beneficent actor in shaping American life. The Industrial Revolution was urbanizing the nation. European immigration was overwhelming cities. Tenements were seen as breeding grounds of all sorts of problems. In this environment, muckrakers, urban planners, and advocates of a better life created a movement to make cities beautiful. Their vision largely depended on the benefits of auto travel.[5]

Henry Ford's Model T made cars accessible to the masses. Between 1913 and 1927, more than 15 million were produced, and auto manufacturing became the biggest industry in America. William C. Durant and Alfred Sloan built General Motors into the model of the modern American corporation and, by the 1950s, into the largest business in the world. There is some evidence that, in the 1930s, GM conspired to buy up streetcar systems and convert them to buses.[6] Regardless of any conspiracy, cars took over American transportation. With them came highways, gas stations, shopping centers, parking lots, and the modern, largely suburban, city.

Phoenix is often described as the "epitome of post–World War II Western auto-oriented suburban development."[7] Yet, uncharacteristically for such a place, Phoenix grew into a big city without a meaningful freeway system. Starting in the 1950s, civic leaders began studying California's experience with freeways and planning for the interstate highway link into Phoenix. In 1967, most areas the size of metro Phoenix carried five times more traffic on freeways.

Historically, the city placed great reliance on the federal government for support of growth, yet it showed a surprising willingness to pass up much of the federal freeway money that was available. In contrast to the area's attitude about water projects, the opportunity to access outside money took second place to fighting about exactly where the freeways should be and what they should look like.

The consequences of the lack of freeways were not felt for many years. Throughout the 1960s and 1970s, as the metropolitan area expanded, it continued to be well served by the forgiving nature of its rectilinear street grid. The grid was easy to expand as needed: farm roads were expanded as subdivisions replaced cotton fields. Little advance planning was necessary, and there was no require-ment for a massive upfront investment in street infrastructure. As the roads were expanded, sewer, water, and other utilities would also be extended, usually paid for by developers.

Eventually, the impact of more people and cars began to take its toll. Traffic congestion continued to increase on the arterial streets, despite constant widening. So eventually, freeways with limited access had to be part of the mix. The initial freeway proposals included a radical design feature: through the heart of the city, crossing Central Avenue, the "Inner Loop" was to be elevated on stilts 100 feet in the air.

Opposition to the plan immediately surfaced. By the late 1960s, urban freeways were a mature enough phenomenon that their neg-ative effects in dividing parts of the city and in seeming to increase, not decrease, traffic congestion were well known. A citizens' group against freeways received support from an unlikely quarter: in late 1972, Eugene Pulliam, the publisher of both the *Arizona Republic* and the *Phoenix Gazette* and arguably the single most influential person in Arizona, decided to launch a crusade against the Inner Loop.

The reasons for Pulliam's attitude were complex. He disliked the elevated design, he distrusted land speculators who were buying in the right-of-way, and he believed freeways had been a nega-tive influence on Los Angeles. But most important, he and his wife, Nina, thought freeways would change the quality of life in Phoenix: "I don't care if we grow in our density pattern all the way to Wickenburg, that would be better than the environmental change to our lifestyle that would occur from a major urban freeway program."[8]

Never before had the establishment in Phoenix been so visibly split on an issue related to growth. The city council and most of the business community supported the freeways but, led by Pulliam, the newspapers were relentless—not only editorializing against the proposal, but running photos of Los Angeles smog and congestion on page 1, day after day.[9] Feeling the pressure, the city council finally agreed to put the issue on a public ballot for an advisory vote in 1973, hoping to get a favorable endorsement before public sentiment eroded further. The Inner Loop was rejected by 58 percent of the voters.

Subsequent freeway-expansion efforts without the freeway on stilts were back on the ballot in 1975 and 1979, and the voters ultimately approved. By finally seeking federal dollars, the Inner Loop, as part of Interstate 10, could be built underground with a park on top.

Not until 1985 did growing traffic congestion convince Maricopa County voters to pass a proposition dedicating a 0.5 percent sales tax for a larger network of freeway construction. At the time the sales tax passed, Phoenix had only seventy miles of freeway, making the metropolitan area dead last in number of freeway miles among the seventy-five largest metropolitan areas in the country.

In March 1989, the region's voters were asked to increase the sales tax dedicated to transportation to 1 percent. Part of the money would be used for an ambitious and complex 103-mile rail system. Ultimately, the plan grew so large as to undermine the already thin support in the electorate, and it was defeated by a three-to-two margin. The voters' message seemed to be explicitly anti-public-transit. The plan was simply too grandiose; it did not appear realistic in a city with such low existing public transit ridership, and most voters could not imagine actually using the system.

The sales tax infusion permitted Phoenix to embark on an aggressive program of freeway expansion. Between 1988 and 1992, the area increased both freeway and major street capacity more than did any other urbanized area in the United States. Phoenix dropped from being the fourth most congested major city to twenty-first.[10]

In 1994, freeway construction was again on the ballot, with public transit as a much less visible part of the package. This time the voters were not very interested in transit, but again soundly defeated the measure because of a perception that the existing freeway building program had been mismanaged. By 1999, Phoenix still had fewer freeway miles than any major city except Miami.[11] The percentage of daily vehicle-miles traveled on freeways increased dramatically during the 1990s, but the city still trails most Western cities in the percentage of travel by freeway.

The delay in building freeways may have actually worked to the advantage of the Phoenix metropolitan area. Continued investment in arterial streets served to offer multiple alternative travel routes in a more robust and less divisive pattern than any freeway system could. Phoenix's arterial streets are among the best in the nation, according to the "Pothole Index," ranking 81 percent better than the US average. Tucson, only 100 miles away, was noted as among the worst in the United States on the pothole index.[12]

The network of well-maintained arterials, coupled with freeways, results in Phoenix being among the least-congested big cities in America. The 2012 Urban Mobility Report of the Texas Transportation Institute puts Phoenix last of the nation's fifteen major metropolitan areas for congestion as measured by hours of delay, and fortieth overall, below much smaller cities.[13]

Phoenix's relatively less-congested traffic situation is largely the historical result of the vast square-mile grid of arterial streets inherited from its agricultural past. In the flat, gridded portion of the metropolitan area, those streets provide a redundant system of north-south and east-west travel. A commuter or traveler encountering a bad traffic jam has readily available alternatives by diverting

Figure 4.1. Transportation corridor in the East Valley—the Superstition Freeway, US Route 60, viewed from above, looking west from Mesa toward Tempe and Phoenix. (© Shutterstock: Tim Roberts Photography)

to other equally large alternative roadways. This grid made it possible for Phoenix to wait before building freeways, and it continues to provide travel alternatives.

In 2000, the residents of the Phoenix metropolitan area decided to approve construction of a light-rail line, called Valley Metro. Success this time was based on a smaller system linking existing activity centers in downtown Tempe and Phoenix. A carefully orchestrated campaign convinced voters that the line would be used and that it would mark Phoenix as a "big city." As authorized, the line is a thirteen-and-a-half-mile route linking Mesa, Tempe, and Phoenix, at a cost of about $1.5 billion. The line was the result of a public vote in which nearly two-thirds of Phoenix voters approved a half-cent sales tax. The proposal included money for an upgrade to the city's relatively inadequate bus system as well as authority to build light rail. Despite some complications in its construction, the light-rail system is now in operation, primarily on city streets where trains move with traffic in a separated center lane.

The Valley Metro system opened at the end of 2008 to great fanfare, with rock bands and street fairs along the route. Rail cars were packed beyond capacity, with 90,000 people riding on the first day.[14] The system immediately became more successful than its original projections. A major part of the success was the coincident move by Arizona State University to build a far more robust student presence in downtown Phoenix. As a result, thousands of ASU students, faculty, and staff ride between the Tempe campus and the new downtown Phoenix campus every day. ASU already had a small presence in downtown Phoenix and would likely have expanded based purely on the city's willingness to invest in buildings for the university. Light rail was clearly a huge benefit to ASU

Figure 4.2. Light rail in downtown Phoenix, serving the downtown ASU campus. (Source: Arizona State University photo, © 2015, Arizona Board of Regents. Used with permission.)

in making it possible for students to actually take classes in both locations.

In 2014, a "sky train" people-mover connection to the airport was created, adding additional ridership. This connection reinforced the huge strategic asset of having an in-town large airport. The system is operating with between 40,000 and 50,000 weekday boardings, on average, beating original estimates for ridership in 2020. Income has actually exceeded the originally stated goal, with about 45 percent operational cost recovery at the fare box. Phoenix's light-rail system has more riders per mile than those of Seattle or San Diego and does significantly better than peer cities with regard to cost recovery.[15]

Part of the justification for light rail, as opposed to an enhanced bus system, was that light rail would spur more private investment along the rail line. The prominence and visibility of light rail, it was believed, coupled with transit-oriented development zoning density along the line, would create incentives for private real estate investment. Valley Metro cites a figure of $7 billion invested near light-rail lines and stations since 2004, though much of that is public development by the City of Phoenix and Arizona State University. A casual ride along the light-rail line is a tour through dozens of four- and five-story, multi-family developments as well as retail and restaurant clusters.

In August of 2015, voters again got a chance to weigh in, this time on a $30-billion transportation plan for the City of Phoenix that would triple the number of light-rail miles, fund bus and street improvements, and add bike lanes, again through a sales tax increase, in this case 0.7 percent, lasting until 2050 (it would replace the existing 0.4 percent tax). Business interests strongly supported "Prop 104." One vocal member of the city council was strongly opposed, as were libertarian-leaning commentators. The election was part of a package of city measures put to the voters in August, a slow time in Phoenix when many people are out of town, and was conducted largely by mail. The vote may not have been a model of participatory democracy, but the proposition carried 55

Figure 4.3. The Skytrain terminal connects light rail to the airport near downtown Phoenix. (Photo by author)

percent to 45 percent among the 20 percent of registered voters who turned out.

The same section-line grid of streets that has served Phoenix so well can provide the backbone of a bus rapid-transit system. It is easy for public-transit users to perceive where they are trying to go and how to get there if they know the direction of every street served by a system. The bus rapid-transit system used in Curitiba, Brazil, is probably the best known in the world and is the kind of infrastructure that would work well in many parts of metropolitan Phoenix. The buses there operate more like rail transit in that they move in a dedicated lane, do not require passengers to pay a fare or interact with the driver when loading, have more doors, and as a result move through a route much more quickly. But because these are buses and not rail lines, they are much less expensive to install. The wide arterials of Phoenix could be retrofitted to accommodate such a bus system. The 2015 ballot proposition includes $17 billion for bus and bus rapid-transit improvements.

Phoenix's experience with light rail has been more successful than anyone expected. This is because the initial link pulled together the most important activity centers in the area: downtown Phoenix and downtown Tempe (each with an ASU campus), sports venues, and Sky Harbor Airport. (This lesson, however, has not fully permeated the Phoenix metropolitan area. The City of Scottsdale, whose downtown is the third walkable urban environment in the area, has resisted the introduction of light rail.) The positive experience is not unique to Phoenix. San Diego, Denver, and Salt Lake City have made major successful rail investments. Los Angeles continues to expand its large system. Most of this growth—to thirty-five light-rail cities in the United States—has included both federal investment and also locally raised taxes.

Because public transit is so dependent on public funding, it must have political acceptance. There is a lesson here from the initially failed "Val Trans" proposal in which Phoenix sought to build a very large, very expensive rail system. It failed because it was too ambitious and too difficult for people to imagine. The Valley Metro light-rail system that was ultimately approved and built is more modest and incremental, and has outpaced projected ridership. With the addition of a linkage to the airport, it has become enormously successful and is likely to gain sufficient public support for expansion. Cities change in increments, and attempts at intentional transformation must respect the pace of those increments.

Another lesson of public transit in a new city is that it will, to a degree, reshape development patterns. A challenge when introducing public transit into an already developed urban area is the temptation to route it to satisfy political constituencies—for example, attempting to link up hoped-for activity centers that may not have any actual need to interact with one another. Another lesson is

Figure 4.4. Light rail has spurred higher-density construction along the route. (Photo by author)

that it is not simply the transit line itself that is the greatest spur to development; it is the location of individual stations.

In the fog of transportation rhetoric, it is important to recognize some clear realities. The existing development pattern of suburban cities essentially requires that every household have some sort of personal vehicle. Nationally, there were 1.8 vehicles per household in 2013.[16] Nearly 90 percent of all US workers drive or are driven to work, with approximately 5 percent taking public transit. The figure for Phoenix is even lower: about 4 percent.[17] For all trips in the United States, not just those for work, only about 6 percent are human powered. Compare this with other industrialized countries like England, where 60 percent of workers walk and bike, or Germany with 34 percent. On an international scale, among American cities only the New York City metro area can compare for public-transit use and walking. New York metro registers 229 transit trips per capita, San Francisco has 131, and no other US metro area has over 100. Phoenix/Mesa has twenty.[18] Americans are slowly changing, however, with 10.8 billion trips in 2014, the highest such figure in fifty-eight years.[19] A need for personal vehicles will likely persist far into the future.

Since nearly every US household has a car, a fair analysis of transportation costs cannot simply compare the costs of driving a car to the costs of riding on public transit. The largest cost of an automobile trip is the capital investment in the automobile. Once that capital investment has been made, an individual consumer's choice is between taking the car or riding on public transit. The incremental cost of using the car is less and the convenience is much greater. This means that rationally behaving consumers living in an environment in which they must have personal vehicles to survive will often continue to favor those personal vehicles.

It is common to associate increased traffic with new development. But the change in lifestyle to one of increasing mobility for all purposes has also substantially contributed to increasing traffic. If the baby boomers had driven as much as did their parents, traffic would have increased by 25 percent when boomers took to the roads. Instead, between 1969 and 1983, traffic increased by 56 percent.[20] Even in areas where population is on the decline, traffic often increases. Part of the reason is the change in working and living patterns—eating out and daily shopping. There is evidence that per capita vehicle-miles traveled is beginning to change slowly with more urban dwellers and an aging population.[21]

Just within the last several years, it has become clear that transportation is undergoing yet another dramatic transformation. Lighter-weight alternative-fuel and electric vehicles are beginning to penetrate the consumer markets. For a long time, in many of the retirement communities in central Arizona, like Sun City, large numbers of residents have used golf carts for neighborhood errands. Some builders even make small garages for neighborhood electric vehicles an option. In Phoenix, with an average commuting distance of about eleven miles, it is increasingly possible for vehicles like the Nissan Leaf or other limited-range electric vehicles to be used by commuters.[22]

The most difficult problem for an automobile-based city in a post-automobile era is what is referred to as "the problem of the last mile." This phrase was originally coined by the telecommunications industry, which recognized that a very high percentage of its capital expense and operating costs was consumed in getting from a hub to individual houses. Similarly, the problem moved into the supply-chain management area, again in recognition of the difficult final leg of a product's journey. Transportation engineers apply the expression with equal accuracy to the dilemma of getting from a transit stop to an individual home or workplace. In a high-density environment like Manhattan, that distance is a few blocks. In a suburban city, that distance is a mile or more. And in a suburban city in a really hot place, walking that last mile is to be avoided. Bicycles, if they can be taken on public-transit vehicles or obtained from a bike-share station, can help, but some people are too old, too dressed up, or simply too lazy to use bikes. Bike-share systems are slowly penetrating urban America, with varied success. GRID Bike Share entered the Phoenix area in late 2014, with 500 bikes in the city of Phoenix and another 500 in Tempe and Mesa.

Today, it appears increasingly likely that the problem of the last mile, and with it the problem of adapting a suburban city into the future, is also likely to be solved by an old standby: technology.

The advent of "smart mobility," which means autonomous or semi-autonomous vehicles, is also likely to be a boon to places like Phoenix with an understandable and easily navigable geography and wide, well-maintained streets. The revolution toward smart mobility is coming more quickly than anyone would have predicted a few years ago. Some public-transit advocates worry that autonomous, fuel-efficient, lightweight vehicles will undercut a desirable move toward mass transit. But for cities that were built on personal-mobility vehicles, smart mobility is likely to be the wave of the future and a critical piece of adapting existing automobile-based urban fabric to a post-petroleum era.

Some of the newest companies in America, such as Apple, Google, and Tesla, are competing with some of the oldest industrial companies in the world, such as Mercedes-Benz, Ford, and General Motors, to create autonomous cars. Self-driving cars offer substantial benefits well beyond "sending guiltless text messages on the way to work."[23] Self-driving cars would allow vehicles to be used in actual trips at a far higher percentage of their time; that is, a driverless car could deliver one family member to a destination and instead of sitting idle for the entire day, drive itself back home to pick up someone else and take them to a different destination. The amount of required parking could be dramatically reduced, freeing up land for higher-density redevelopment. Researchers at MIT's SENSEable City Laboratory estimate that, in some locations, it would be possible to take every passenger to his or her destination with 80 percent fewer cars. Autonomous cars also might mean fewer people getting lost and, arguably, therefore less congestion. But if those autonomous vehicles are being much more heavily utilized, actual travel would not diminish.

Even before driverless vehicles become available, we are already seeing a transportation revolution based on the ability to purchase transportation one trip at a time. Uber and Lyft are challenging one of the least innovative and most entrenched service industries in America—taxi cabs—to the point of rendering them largely obsolete.

Uber began in 2009 as luxury car service in San Francisco by which cars could be summoned with a smart phone. In four years, it had a million riders a day and could be accessed by 55 percent of

Figure 4.5. *Autonomous vehicle with GPS and radar driving on the road.*
(© *Shutterstock: Martial Red*)

the US population. As a business model, it exploded as fast as any company in history, largely based on word of mouth.[24] (However, the story did have an occasional dark side of allegedly predatory business practices and arguable exploitation of workers as "independent contractors.")

Uber arrived in Phoenix relatively early and has received strong political support. Governor Doug Ducey championed Uber as a twenty-first-century technology and early in his administration signed legislation legalizing ride-sharing companies like Uber and Lyft. In the summer of 2015, Uber opened a significant office in downtown Phoenix, aiming at 300 employees.

The incredible growth of Uber is testament to a stunning revolution in transportation systems. Buying transportation by the trip, and covering even the "last mile" that way, is radically different and transformative. Taxi service is an example of an entrenched, obsolete business model protected by archaic anti-competitive regulations. Even just serving late-night customers leaving restaurants and bars has become an explosive business model in the age of tough drunk-driving laws. Uber's model goes farther—it brings taxi-like on-demand services to places that never had decent service. If ultimately coupled with autonomous vehicles, "Uberish" services could become the Internet of the physical world.

It is also increasingly possible to solve some transportation problems with non-transportation solutions. The availability of ubiquitous Internet access has made it possible to significantly reduce the necessity of rush-hour commuting, since the size of most of the big streets in American cities is dictated by morning and evening peak-travel movements. Shaving rush-hour traffic can have a impact on travel times, street design, and the quality of life for millions of commuters. More people are working from home one or more days every week. There are examples of CEOs who live in Santa Fe supervising employees based in Los Angeles and of virtual offices where workers live wherever they want, interact electronically, and meet occasionally.

There was a time, early in the Internet age, when it appeared that physical interaction for work would diminish so dramatically that the need for urban environments themselves might decline, with people returning to bucolic rural settings with great electronic connectivity. Evidence today suggests this will not be the case. Even those self-employed millennials who do not need, want, or have an office to go to still seek face-to-face meetings and human interaction. They go to a coffee shop or a co-working environment and behave the way people used to in offices. The city of the future is not a place without gathering places, concentrations, and nodes of activity. To the contrary, those sorts of "punctuation marks" in the urban fabric seem to be increasing, not decreasing.

It is not hard to imagine a future in which the city of Phoenix has an expanded and more robust light-rail system, a series of bus rapid-transit routes, and an autonomous-vehicle network serving most people's transportation needs. Sharing the road with these systems would, of course, be a continuing cohort of conventional automobiles powered by petroleum, electricity, or a combination of the two. We are on the edge of a transportation revolution as profound as that of the railroad or the automobile. At the brink of dramatic technological change, it is impossible to fully anticipate the impact of that change on physical and social environments. These sweeping technological changes are driven by a need to adapt the resource consumption of today's world to a different future. They are also driven by a need to sustain an existing urban fabric based on the automobile. Coupled with older technologies—light rail, streetcar, and bus—and with the increasing densification of suburban cities, a sustainable future will evolve.

Chapter 5

Houses, Shopping Centers, and the Fabric of Suburbia

Examinations of phoenix tend to begin in the air. That is where *Phoenix in Perspective* starts its narrative. Works by Michael Sorkin and Alex Shoumatoff do likewise. Sorkin writes that "inky emptiness abuts the grid of lights, the desert lapping at the edges of town."[1] When *Newsweek* examined the phenomenon of the suburbs in May of 1995, it began with an aerial view of Phoenix as a way to capture the boundless sense of space.[2] Flying into Phoenix graphically reveals a metropolis that sits as an island in the middle of an inhospitable sea of creosote, cactus, and venomous creatures.

The isolation of the metropolis conveys the reality of the urban West. As the Brookings Institution has noted, the intermountain West is the most urban part of the United States, measured by the percentage of residents living in cities.[3] The Midwestern and Eastern pattern of small towns, villages, and family farms is largely absent "beyond the hundredth meridian," where irrigated agriculture has

Figure 5.1. Phoenix city lights at dusk. (© Shutterstock: Gill Couto)

concentrated population centers. The different settlement pattern of the American West is a largely misunderstood phenomenon in the dialogue about sustainability and makes direct comparisons between Western cities and Eastern cities difficult.

Phoenix itself was the last of the big Western cities to experience a boom in population growth.[4] As the United States expanded westward, the legendary "frontier line" largely skipped over the Southwestern desert to arrive in California with the Gold Rush. Denver, too, experienced early population growth based on a nineteenth-century boom in mining. When Brigham Young founded Salt Lake City in 1847 with a sense of religious imperative, Phoenix barely existed as an identifiable location. Tucson and Santa Fe were both grounded in a similar if less expansive religious context based on Spanish mission settlements reaching up from Mexico.

Phoenix's generally accepted modern history begins in 1867, when Jack Swilling realized that the Salt River Valley offered farmland free of rocks and frost. Swilling was a classic Western hero (or antihero): a former Confederate soldier and deserter, a Union Army freighter and scout, a prospector, a farmer, a speculator, a drunk, a scoundrel. By 1868, diverted water from the Salt River was flowing in his ditch. Most accounts hold that it was Darrell Duppa, a similarly colorful Eastern expat, who suggested the name "Phoenix" as suitable for the new town "springing from the ruins" of the civilization of the Hohokam.[5]

The completion of the rail link in 1887 and the opening of a firebrick factory made conventional building materials available. The city's boosters wanted the buildings of Phoenix to look more "American," and so brick and wood structures began to replace adobe in popularity. The settlement was platted in a square-mile grid in 1876. In this, Phoenix followed early American town models where preplanning of city form was made possible by available land and an expectation of settlement. The efficiency of the grid was especially well suited to flatlands and non-port locations, where the center of town was simply the intersection of two streets.

Throughout its infancy, Phoenix grew steadily but did not boom. There were still too many impediments to growth. The river was unpredictable, and more irrigation works and storage areas were needed to stabilize the water supply. So, at the turn of the century, population statistics dramatically reflected these differences: Denver, 134,000; Salt Lake City, 53,000; El Paso, 16,000; Phoenix, 5,500.

At the turn of the twentieth century, Phoenix finally began to grow, largely pushed by the kind of classic civic boosters that populated American boomtowns with a goal of luring newcomers in order to drive up the value of real estate. Decades earlier, when Tocqueville traveled to the American frontier, he passed through these boomtowns and observed that "an American changes his residence ceaselessly."[6] These newly built boomtowns were practical contrivances to be started, built up, sold, and adapted. Phoenix in this era was populated by citizens who had migrated there in search of a better life and became boosters of the Phoenix lifestyle.

The attachment of this kind of leader to a place is very different than that of a third-generation Boston Brahman. The goal is not to maintain or preserve but to build.

The idea that cities should develop in an orderly, planned, and regulated fashion became predominant in the 1920s with the advent of zoning ordinances. Zoning principally began as an attempt to reduce crowding and bring light and air to the tenements of New York City, and to separate industrial areas from residences. After the US Supreme Court validated the practice as a constitutional use of the police power in 1926, zoning ordinances multiplied across the country.[7]

Throughout the growing Southwest and Southern California, zoning was quickly seized upon by real estate entrepreneurs as a means of stabilizing property values by ensuring that entire areas would develop consistently. Zoning became a tool to limit undesirable uses and populations to certain parts of town. Previously, the only control available was through deed restrictions imposed on land by the owner. Using zoning, developers could extend their vision of a consistent, homogeneous community onto their neighbors' property.

During the 1920s, housing development began to move beyond simple preparation of lots to marketing, promotion, and delivery of finished homes. Building a house on speculation became a marketing tool, allowing potential buyers the possibility of viewing their prospective investment in all its splendor.

The evolution of Phoenix homebuilders from contractors of individual houses to developers came early. This phenomenon is generally thought to have originated largely in California, though most development in Los Angeles continued to separate homebuilding from lot development until well into the 1930s.[8] By 1927, several builder-driven subdivisions existed in Phoenix.

The transition from single-lot sales into actual home construction was simple economics. A subdivider who obtains plat approval and installs streets and utilities is called in industry jargon a "horizontal developer." This type of work requires capital more than labor. Early in the twentieth century it therefore came to be dominated by bankers, real estate agents, and businessmen. A horizontal developer assumes the costs of owning the land and the expense of constructing streets and infrastructure.[9] He hopes to sell lots to homebuilders (or "vertical developers") as quickly as possible. Homebuilders were often undercapitalized tradesmen-carpenters and masons who built a few houses each year. In order to get a vertical builder to buy the lots, the horizontal developer had to offer a number of concessions, such as a very low down payment and no carrying costs for several months. The homebuilder's financial commitment was thereby limited, but the land developer was incurring an increasing level of obligation with no cash flow—in effect, subsidizing the individual homebuilder. It was a natural economic move for the lot developers to move into the homebuilding business, integrating the horizontal and vertical components of residential development.

Coincident with the rise of the homebuilder-developer in Phoenix was a growing concern at the federal level that there was a crisis in American homeownership. Between 1890 and 1930, the proportion of Americans who owned their own homes had risen from 36 percent to 47 percent. But the Depression reversed the trend, and by 1940 only 41 percent were homeowners.[10] This small change was viewed as the beginning of an alarming trend, reversing decades of progress. As a result, under the Coolidge Administration, Secretary of Commerce Herbert Hoover was made chairman of the Better Homes in America Commission. Coolidge explained the need for such a movement: "The American home is the foundation of our national and individual well-being."[11]

In 1931, the President's Conference on Home Building and Home Ownership set the framework for many of the Roosevelt Administration's New Deal policies: replacement of short-term mortgages with long-term amortized mortgages, federally backed loans, and reduced homebuilding costs through large-scale residential development and standardized building practices. By absolutely asserting a new American truth—that ownership of the single-family detached home was an American birthright—these policies became the most influential set of government actions ever to affect the space and character of American cities.

Ultimately, federal involvement in homebuilding dramatically increased the percentage of American homeowners. These policies spurred more efficient construction techniques, as had been hoped. With government oversight, construction experimentation—especially to reduce cost—was encouraged. Design experimentation, on the other hand, was not.

As entrepreneurs, the Phoenicians of the first part of the twentieth century hoped that the combination of sunshine and cheap land would attract large numbers of new citizens. They had come to view real estate profit itself as the motivating force for growth. The realization that development could be an industry all on its own came to Phoenix at about the same time it was recognized in Los Angeles. This notion was something new to city building: a future driven not by migration to employment locations, but rather by developers motivated by profit who would seek out both employers and residents.[12] Between 1900 and 1930, the population of Los Angeles exploded from this formula, growing by a factor of ten. But having the vision was not the same thing as achieving it. Los Angeles had attractions that Phoenix lacked: temperate summers, an ocean, the Rose Parade. To most Americans, the desert Southwest remained a foreign and inhospitable place, useful as a movie set and a refuge for eccentrics, but not as a place to live.

World War II transformed Phoenix through air travel and air-conditioning. Despite the efforts of its leading citizens, Phoenix's rail link to the rest of the country never turned the city into a major transportation hub. Commercial air travel had a different result. Lodged inside a silver fuselage, one could avoid the hostility and isolation of the desert simply by leaping over it. In November 1928, a company called Scenic Airways bought an airfield two miles east of downtown, between 24th and 32nd Streets, and named it Sky

Harbor. The name invoked the future of air travel: airplanes would perform the age-old port function that desert cities had always lacked. Other commercial carriers joined in using this facility, and the city acquired the airport in 1935.[13]

The war became an enormous magnet that attracted Americans to California and Texas to work in defense-related industries. During the 1940s, nearly every new Westerner was an urban dweller drawn by war industries. As the huge defense complex began looking for civilian business opportunities, electronics manufacturing companies realized that with air travel, manufacturing plants could locate away from conventional transportation routes. The new commercial airlines were looking for goods and people to transport. Passenger travel by air exploded after the war, from fewer than 600,000 passengers in 1934 to nearly 15 million in 1948.[14]

A train can make multiple stops with relative efficiency and little incremental additional expense. In air travel, multiple stops are to be avoided because of the penalty in cost and delay. Speed is the benefit of travel by air, and that benefit is greatest with fewer stops. So air travel had the effect of concentrating business activity in fewer, larger cities with substantial airports. Those cities became dominant centers of regional areas, with the big airport being the hub of other transportation modes.

As air travel grew and air-conditioning began to penetrate the housing market, metropolitan Phoenix finally found its boom. As that happened, the City of Phoenix itself sought to expand. Annexation became a vital part of the City's strategy. By the mid-twentieth century, the plight of many Eastern urban areas was becoming clear: growth on the edge was attracting the new suburban homeowners. A middle-class wage earner who would have been a lifetime renter before the war was able, with government-backed financing, to purchase a home for the first time. New suburban homes were being built rapidly and efficiently.

In well-established urban areas, this emerging pattern of homeownership meant that many rural communities were being transformed into bedroom suburbs. The established big city was often landlocked by smaller existing municipalities or by natural boundaries such as rivers, lakes, or coasts. Suburban growth became a drain on the central city, which began a gradual demographic decline. With that decline came an erosion of revenues.

Phoenix faced a different reality. The city's prewar downtown, such as it was, was that of a small Midwestern city. Nor did Phoenix have either geographic or political boundaries to keep it from expanding. Watching what was happening around the country, the city's leadership realized that they had a choice. They could allow the city of Phoenix to be surrounded by satellites that might grow at its expense, or embark on a campaign of aggressive annexation in order to expand. The existing cities of Tempe, Scottsdale, Mesa, and Glendale did create some limits, but those communities were themselves able to expand through annexation. In other directions, especially to the north, Phoenix had a clear path to extend its geographic borders. Beginning in 1956, the elected officials of Phoenix set out on a conscious course to avoid being hemmed in by a group of independent suburbs.[15] In 1940, Phoenix had covered an area of 9.6 square miles. By 1955, it covered 29 square miles, and by 1960, 187 square miles. The annexation program was so aggressive that by 1960, 75 percent of the people living in the city limits were residents of areas that had been annexed in the previous ten years.

The two most pervasive postwar building forms in American architecture were the shopping center and the ranch house. Together, these building forms changed the nature of how cities grew and what they looked like. Shopping centers and ranch houses became the building blocks of metropolitan Phoenix and the suburban cities of the modern West.

Exactly what constitutes a shopping center, as opposed to a collection of individual shops, is open to interpretation. Today, the commonly accepted definition requires a group of architecturally unified buildings built on a site that is planned, developed, and managed as a single entity.[16] Historically, the distinguishing characteristic of a shopping center has been highly visible and accessible parking shared by several different stores. When shopping became a motorized rather than a pedestrian activity, storefronts were ultimately pushed away from the street because the visibility of parking became more of an attraction than the visibility of merchandise. That single design change transformed the physical appearance of entire communities.

In Phoenix, an infatuation with visible surface parking came remarkably early, in the late 1920s. When the A. J. Bayless market chain opened its seventh store in March 1928, it set the building back thirty-five feet from the curb line in order to provide ample parking room for "several score" automobiles in a "provision which thus has been made for motoring shoppers [which] will prevent congestion of parked machines in [the] streets near the store."[17]

Bayless's new market was 8,000 square feet in size, the largest it had ever built and a good example of a growing phenomenon— the supermarket. From an early Piggly Wiggly self-service store in Memphis in 1916, the supermarket spread across America.[18] After World War I, the average household was able to acquire a refrigerator, an appliance that revolutionized shopping habits. A housewife equipped with a refrigerator, and later with a freezer, was freed from having to shop every day. A weekly shopping trip meant there were too many bags to be carried at once, and a car was necessary to transport the groceries. The necessary parking meant that large supermarkets were not suited to downtown locations.

The supermarket became the anchor of the shopping center, which added an assortment of other often-frequented shopping destinations, all of which could be visited on a single trip. As suburban housing began to boom, the shopping center became an integral part of growth. In 1950, there were only 100 neighborhood shopping centers in the United States. By 1953, the number had tripled, and by 1960, there were 3,700.[19]

As Phoenix began its rapid annexation program, the national trend toward business and retail decentralization was in full swing. The intersections of two section-line arterial roads provided perfect locations for dispersed retail shopping centers, gas stations, and convenience restaurants. A development pattern began to emerge—a developer would acquire a quarter section or more of land and subdivide it for houses, holding out a ten-acre parcel on the corner for a shopping center. A commercial developer, often with a supermarket anchor tenant already committed, would build the center several years later. By 1957, aerial photos of the city of Phoenix make this pattern clear: at least two dozen section-line corner shopping centers are in operation, with at least as many vacant sites surrounded by subdivisions.[20]

It is tempting but inaccurate to think of the growth that occurred in the suburban cities of the Southwest in the 1950s and 1960s as being unprecedented in American history. In fact, between 1850 and 1890, Chicago grew from 29,000 people to more than 1 million. The difference was that the post–World War II growth of Phoenix and the urban Southwest was accommodated in the lower-density urban fabric of dispersed employment and retail and, above all, of detached single-family homes.

World War II had necessarily put concerns about home ownership on hold. Housing starts during the war years fell from 1 million nationally to fewer than 100,000.[21] Rising birth rates and returning GIs put enormous demands on housing after the war, and the speed and efficiency that had been applied to war production provided new lessons for homebuilders. Easy financing programs under the Federal Housing Administration and the Veterans Administration, in combination with the attention paid to new home construction by popular magazines, architects, and manufacturers, spurred the largest increase in homebuilding in American history.

FHA and VA mortgages were also designed to keep houses within reach of as many Americans as possible. Immediately after the war, returning GIs and the families they established expected to be able to buy houses. They even had an expectation about cost: about two years' wages—around $5,000 to $6,000.[22]

The houses, which would become the units of production, needed to be simple, efficient, easy to build in volume, and suited to families with automobiles. The evolution into integrated land development and homebuilding had proven successful, and it was this developer-driven model that was able to meet postwar demand. Developers wanted home designs that required little architectural input after the initial design. To the problem of providing houses in large numbers, a new science was applied: market research. Between 1936 and 1950, dozens of large-scale consumer housing surveys were run by the mass-market family and ladies' magazines.[23] These surveys looked at citizens as consumers and houses as products. They revealed that people wanted yards with a place for the kids to play, kitchens that opened to the rest of the home, and an informal "family room" where children could be comfortable and the television could be the focus of family life. Bedrooms should be separate private zones, and more than one bathroom was expected.[24] When these preferences for a more open floor plan and private yard merged with the need for efficient low-cost production, a suitable style emerged—the ranch house.

The ranch house was in part a repudiation of the make-believe world of period-revival housing. The harsh reality of World War II had brought everyone back to understanding the need for simple, inexpensive housing. Ranch-style architecture was deeply rooted in the Western soil and well adapted to the Western climate. It is probable that the earliest adaptations of ranch house form to modern housing appeared in the early 1930s in both Southern and Northern California.[25] The early prototypes were related to the California bungalow style as well as to the vernacular Spanish rural house. The houses were one-story, with a low-pitched roof, generous overhangs, and simple construction materials. Outdoor living areas were integrated, "underscoring the important principle of providing an easy relationship with the out-of-doors."[26]

At the same time that the individual ranch house's design was being refined for mass marketing, the policies of the FHA were also influencing the larger context of neighborhood planning. The FHA's standards moved beyond individual buildings to the relationship of these buildings to one another, with the notion that a streetscape should present an appearance of uniformity and design continuity so as to uphold property values.[27] This planning concept was a continuation of the efforts of the FHA to standardize building practices and to reduce costs. It was also indicative of the shift that occurred in the role of the developer from land subdivider to community builder—the first of whom, in Phoenix, was John F. Long.

In 1947, as a returning veteran, Long built a single house for himself and his wife, Mary. Even before they could move in, they were offered a price that represented a profit of nearly 50 percent, and they sold it for $8,000. Within two years, Long had become a tract-home builder. By 1952, a Phoenix FHA official called Long's houses "the best value in town," and another FHA man in Washington said that "no one in the country can touch him."[28]

In 1953, Long assembled 2,000 acres in twenty tracts for a planned community he named Maryvale after his wife. He hired Los Angeles architect and planner Victor Gruen to lay out a master plan, which included schools, parks, employment areas, and shopping centers. The community opened in 1955 with a carnival-like event called "The Greatest Home Show on Earth." Billboards heralded three-bedroom, two-bath homes for $7,950, and homes with swimming pools for $9,800. Eventually Maryvale grew to house 100,000 people.

Figure 5.2. The grand opening of Maryvale. (Photo courtesy of John F. Long Properties)

Long's Maryvale is a preeminent example of the suburban development that symbolize American life of the 1950s and 1960s. While numerous social critics "gleefully lambasted ranch-house developments as the tasteless hallmark of a homogenized society," most of the new suburban dwellers were happy with the homes they bought.[29] The ranch-house suburbs brought home ownership to a broader range of Americans than ever before—and made it a defining characteristic of middle-class status. Mass-production techniques kept homes affordable and created the new phenomenon of the "starter home." The young families of the 1950s looked forward to increased buying power as they matured, assuming (correctly, it turned out) that they would move on to newer and larger houses rather than staying in place, as previous generations had done. Houses were simply one more part of their lives as increasingly affluent consumers.[30]

Throughout this period of growth, the City of Phoenix continued its aggressive annexation policies to absorb new development, and in 1997 the city's 469 square miles surpassed the total size of Los Angeles, making Phoenix eighth in geographic size in the nation. Residents of metropolitan Phoenix became accustomed to hearing that the area was either number one or two nationally in single-family housing permits, and often near the top in retail and industrial permitting as well. At various times, Scottsdale, Chandler, Mesa, or Gilbert might be the single fastest-growing city in America.

From World War II through the end of the 1990s, Phoenix's fast growth trajectory set in place its current urban form. The dominance of the automobile and the single-family home meant that, throughout all of America, city populations were dispersed. In older industrial "hub and spoke" cities, these new pressures resulted in redistributing a higher-density population into a more sprawling urban form at lower density. Thus, a city like Philadelphia lost a third of its population while doubling the size of its urban area.[31] For Phoenix and the other postwar American cities, the automobile and the single-family home set the pattern for new population growth in a lower-density, more spread-out environment.

At the same time, the forces of water supply, air travel, and federal land were shaping the growth of Phoenix. The result of these countervailing forces is the urban form of Phoenix today. That form is not remarkably low-density, as is sometimes assumed. The residential density of the Phoenix metropolitan area is about 3,200 people per square mile—higher than that of Seattle, Houston, Charlotte, or Atlanta. Las Vegas, another classic suburban city, is

Table 5.1. Residential Density of Major Metropolitan Regions

Metropolitan Area	Household/Residential Acre
Los Angeles–Long Beach–Santa Ana (CA) MSA	3.85
Las Vegas–Paradise (NV) MSA	3.72
San Jose–Sunnyvale–Santa Clara (CA)	3.66
San Francisco–Oakland–Fremont (CA) MSA	3.24
New York–Northern New Jersey–Long Island (NY-NJ-PA) MSA	3.21
Miami–Fort Lauderdale–Pompano Beach (FL) MSA	3.16
San Diego–Carlsbad–San Marcos (CA)	2.85
Denver–Aurora–Broomfield (CO) MSA	2.64
Salt Lake City (UT) MSA	2.59
Tampa–St. Petersburg–Clearwater (FL) MSA	2.57
Chicago–Joliet–Naperville (IL-IN-WI) MSA	2.46
Philadelphia–Camden–Wilmington (PA-NJ-DE-MD) MSA	2.36
Boston–Cambridge–Quincy (MA-NH) MSA	2.32
Dallas–Fort Worth–Arlington (TX) MSA	2.23
Phoenix–Mesa–Glendale (AZ) MSA	2.19
Seattle–Tacoma–Bellevue (WA) MSA	2.17
Washington–Arlington–Alexandria (DC-VA-MD-WV) MSA	2.16
Houston–Sugar Land–Baytown (TX) MSA	2.06
Charlotte–Gastonia–Rock Hill (NC-SC) MSA	1.96
Detroit–Warren–Livonia (MI) MSA	1.89
Riverside–San Bernardino–Ontario (CA) MSA	1.62
Atlanta–Sandy Springs–Marietta (GA) MSA	1.57

Source: Center for Neighborhood Technology, Housing + Transportation Index, 2011.

actually one of the densest metro areas in the United States at 4,500 people per square mile (see table 5.1). The highest-density metropolitan area overall is Los Angeles, at 7,000 people per square mile.[32]

What is remarkable about places like Phoenix, Las Vegas, and Los Angeles is not that they are extremely low-density but rather that their density has been more uniform from the downtown area to the edge than is the case in older metropolitan areas like New York, Boston, and Chicago. In Phoenix, for example, close to the downtown area most people are living on 5,000- to 6,000-square-foot lots. Twenty-five miles from the downtown area, in the distant suburbs of Phoenix, people are living on 5,000- to 6,000-square-foot lots.

The Metropolitan Policy Program at the Brookings Institution has looked at America's newest metropolitan places in its study of "mountain megas." In analyzing the growth of the Sun Corridor, the Phoenix/Tucson area, Brookings concludes that Arizona's megapolitan region has grown relatively densely and is one of the most-efficient new urban areas in terms of urbanizing raw land. The region converted land to urban use at the rate of 0.148 acre of rural land for every new housing unit between 1980 and 2000. In the lower forty-eight states, the average conversion rate was more than 2.0 acres.[33] This is the result of the fact that most growth in the Phoenix metropolitan area takes place on the immediate edge of the city rather than leapfrogging far out into rural areas, and this new growth is built out at relatively high densities on small, single-family lots.

The Sun Corridor offers interesting comparisons to other competitive megapolitan regions. The following figures show the simplistic comparison of population to the size of the megapolitan area just based on a number of counties. When a more refined analysis is done by looking at the actual census tracts with urban-type populations, it becomes clear how different the Sun Corridor is. Eighty-five percent of the population of the Sun Corridor is squeezed onto 5 percent of the land. That 85 percent has a density that is significantly higher than a similar population in Seattle and twice the density of Atlanta or St. Louis.

There is also a tendency to toss off a critique of the new cities of late-twentieth-century America as being "unplanned." This criticism is based in the assumption that such places grew with very little regulatory oversight purely in response to technology, economic forces, and whatever developers felt like building. In fact, the cities of postwar America were relentlessly regulated through

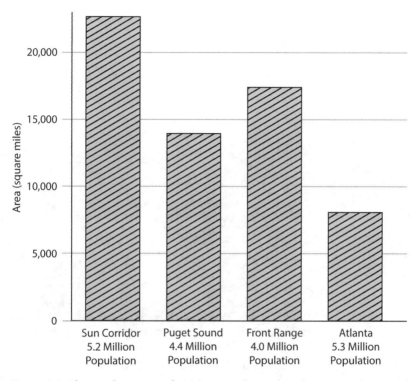

Figure 5.3. The simplistic view of comparative density based on county limits and populations. The Sun Corridor appears the least dense.

zoning, subdivision, and building controls. Urban areas that grew before the mid-1920s did so with a very small set of regulations, usually relating mainly to access for fire equipment or the maximum height of buildings. As zoning controls became prominent in the late 1920s, most new development went through extensive regulatory oversight by municipalities. Los Angeles first began using zoning in a foresightful way to regulate the use of previously undeveloped property as early as 1909. It is historically inaccurate to criticize places like Los Angeles and Phoenix as being unplanned. One may today think they should have been planned differently, but they are largely the result of attitudes about growth, development, and planning at the time they grew.

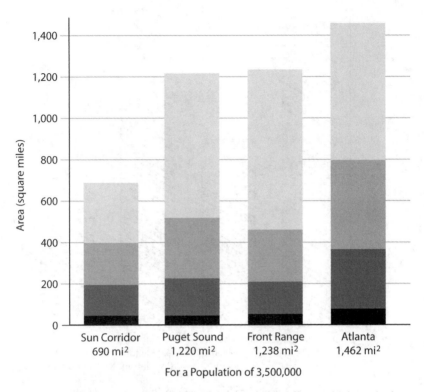

Figure 5.4. The more "realistic" view of density. Each different shade in the bars represents 1 million people. The Sun Corridor is actually the densest megapolitan area here, based on how people actually live. (Source: Dan Hunting, Morrison Institute for Public Policy, ASU)

Phoenix has suffered for decades from its lack of a big-city downtown. Today, many of the city's planning efforts are focused on trying to create such a downtown. As Phoenix began its dramatic growth curve, its old downtown was left behind by the evolution of shopping centers and regional malls. This paralleled a national trend in which new department stores were built only as mall anchors. Regional mall locations were dictated by major stores studying the demography of an area and determining an appropriate trade area.

In early 1974, the Phoenix Planning Commission held a retreat to discuss how best to deal with the continued development of regional shopping locations and dispersed employment. The goal was not to discourage malls, but rather to encourage, anticipate, and plan for such development. The commission invited representatives of the shopping center industry, and one developer paid for the gathering (which ultimately caused a minor scandal). The planning construct that emerged from the meeting has been part of the city's official growth policy ever since: the urban village concept. The city would be divided into villages, initially nine, each with a village core containing regional shopping and employment. Near the retail and employment center would be multi-family housing. Surrounding this core would be a gradient of decreasing development intensity. Finally, near the edge of the village would be lower-density, single-family subdivisions. Each village was to be "relatively self-sufficient in providing living, working, and recreational opportunities for residents."[34]

Phoenix's official decision for the city to be multi-centered has been widely examined. Tony Downs, in *New Visions for Metropolitan America*, recognizes Phoenix as one of the most fully realized visions of the multi-centered network city due to its relatively weak downtown.[35] Joel Garreau similarly profiles the phenomenon in his book *Edge City*.[36]

The reality of organizing the City of Phoenix into anything resembling a series of villages proved difficult to implement. Most of the "cores" consisted of a regional shopping center surrounded by a sea of surface parking, a few low-rise office buildings, and some nearby apartments. Most Phoenix residents did not even realize they lived in an "urban village." The truth was that they moved from one place to another without any recognition of what was supposed to be their logical employment and recreation pattern.

Prior to the advent of village cores, the City of Phoenix limited the area outside of downtown in which high-rise office buildings (defined at that time as anything taller than four stories) could be built to a corridor along Central Avenue, from the downtown to

Camelback Road. Even within that area, proposals to build high-rises were typically met with great resistance by nearby single-family homeowners. Many felt the buildings would loom over their backyards, block their views of mountains, or reflect so much heat and light into their neighborhoods as to lower their property values.[37] Tall buildings were an urban form many people had moved to Phoenix to escape, and having them nearby was not acceptable. Even today, this sentiment persists in most neighborhoods.

By 1980, Phoenix and the metropolitan area it anchored had achieved a long-held goal: the area had become one of America's major metropolitan areas. The formula of automobiles, shopping centers, single-family homes, and air travel had transformed what was often called "the Valley of the Sun" into a prototype of the suburban city. In that same period, a host of other Sunbelt cities arose based on this same formula. The great Texas cities of Houston and Dallas–Fort Worth had been joined by San Antonio and Austin. Tucson had grown, though not nearly as fast as Phoenix, hampered by a less robust water supply and sketchy air travel. Orange County and the inland empire of Riverside–San Bernardino became suburban cities as part of the endless Southern California megapolitan area. Outside of the Sunbelt, a series of other suburban cities had burgeoned across the United States. These places had followed the pattern of the American boomtowns of the frontier and had multiplied quickly in the postwar era based on the new suburban lifestyle. Older American cities had similarly seen their development pattern shift away from denser urban form to spreading out on the fringe. Places like Atlanta had sprawled well outside of the original outline.

As suburban life became the dominant settlement pattern of the United States and continued to flourish throughout the latter decades of the twentieth century, the consequences of the suburban pattern became more and more clear. Increased traffic, social alienation, economic segregation, and environmental degradation are all, to various degrees, legitimately seen as by-products of low-density living, just as, in an earlier era, high-density tenements were seen as squalid, unhealthy, and conducive to crime. How to restructure the suburban fabric to mitigate some of its negative consequences, while still responding to market demands, became a hot topic of conversation at the turn of the twenty-first century.

In the early 1990s, the Congress for the New Urbanism (CNU) was founded by a coalition of architects, urban designers, planners, engineers, journalists, public servants, and concerned citizens. Its goal was to promote a different way of thinking about communities, focused on diversity of use and population, capacity for supporting mass transit, connectivity between neighborhoods, and a rethinking of the relationship between houses, the street, and commercial uses. To the New Urbanists, the vanishing rhythms of small-town life seemed preferable to the modern suburban lifestyle. Consequently, New Urbanists have been criticized for overindulging in an idealistic nostalgia. But many of the principles of New Urbanism have been embraced by development throughout the country, including infill locations and even in new outlying developments in suburban cities. On the edges of Phoenix, for example, both Verrado and Eastmark have elements of New Urbanism: short blocks, planting strips next to streets, pocket parks, and even front porches on houses.

Whether it is seen as "New Urbanism" or "neo-traditional" town planning, the movement is largely about one thing: walking. Suburban cities that were built around the automobile are generally not great places to walk. Even in an environment as rigorously planned as Phoenix, walkability suffers. While almost all streets include sidewalks, and connectivity of neighborhoods is good, and lot sizes are relatively small, the problem is a simple one: there is just not much reason to walk. Commercial sites are far apart and are often separated by parking lots. Even going from one commercial site to another within a single big-box center can mean walking in such a hostile, hot, unshaded, and bleak environment that most people will get in their car and drive around the mall from the Costco to Home Depot. Individual residential neighborhoods are pleasant places to walk, and during the temperate part of the year they teem with activity—people walking their dogs, or children playing, or residents exercising with their FitBits. But the New Urbanist ideal of walking to shop or walking to work is a relatively unusual phenomenon in suburban cities.

In metro Phoenix, however, a few pockets of lively urbanisms have begun to emerge, based on the concept of walking or strolling as an activity. The strolling may be between art galleries and bars, as in downtown Scottsdale, or just between bars, as in downtown Tempe, or among antiques stores, restaurants, and bars, as in downtown Glendale, or among an eclectic mix of local merchants and bars, as in the Roosevelt Row area of downtown Phoenix. In the far-distant Phoenix suburb of Gilbert, a tiny historic downtown is now being revitalized and in some measure re-created with new development. Most of these destinations remain places that one drives to (or in the case of downtown Phoenix and Tempe, perhaps takes light rail) for the sole purpose of walking around and interacting with other people in an urban context. In each case, it appears that the attraction of such an area is beginning to spur residential demand close enough to participate easily in the pedestrian environment. The most-visible examples of high-density in fill residential development have appeared in Scottsdale and Tempe, where thousands of rental and for-sale multi-family units have been built since the turn of the twenty-first century. Many of these were initially planned as condos, but turned out to be too expensive for the market and were transitioned to rentals, or, in Tempe, to student housing. Even downtown Phoenix has experienced a surge of higher-density residential development.

The creation of urban pedestrian contexts in suburban cities is one of the newest hallmarks of development. Places like Santana Row in San Jose represent highlights of this trend. In Scottsdale, the "Old Town" area has been revitalized with new development along the canal banks, including high-rise condos, and a new shopping

Figures 5.5 and 5.6. On one corner, a church and school have been converted to a restaurant and retail site, with a newly built Starbucks. On the same intersection, a former gas station serves enchiladas and soup. (Photos by author)

destination called Kierland Commons was created in the north part of the city. Entirely the product of one developer's vision, it represents the new open "Main Street" style of shopping.

Some of these attempts to create an urban atmosphere have an unfortunate "Disneyland" quality because all the buildings are new and essentially vary only in fenestration and canopy design. But they nonetheless recognize a genuine desire of people to stroll, people-watch, window-shop, sip coffee, grab a beer, and make connections. It is only a short leap to deciding that living in such an environment might be the best idea of all. In the 1980s and 1990s, city planners sought to encourage adding high-density residential to Phoenix "village cores." At first, these ideas were generally scoffed at by developers. But by the early 2000s—before the recession—a market for housing in proximity to shopping and entertainment was definitely emerging.

The future of an urban form built primarily around detached single-family homes is very much in question today. Most attempts to rate cities for sustainability, as well as many commentators on city planning, leap quickly to the conclusion that the city dominated by single-family homes cannot continue. Coupled with the intellectual critique of the suburbs is a repeated analysis of trends purporting to show that baby boomers and millennials are rapidly moving back into higher-density urban places.

Nevertheless, the single-family-home-dominated tableau remains a dominant urban form throughout the United States and increasingly throughout the world. The US Census Bureau estimates that, nationwide, only 26 percent of the housing stock is in multi-unit buildings; in Phoenix, the proportion is 23 percent.[38] Joel Kotkin has been the most consistent debunker of the myth that huge numbers of Americans are suddenly seeking a more traditional lifestyle and eschewing the single-family home. As the executive editor of NewGeography.com, Kotkin and his colleague Wendell Cox have written extensively about the realities of continuing urban growth in America.[39] Based on census data, their conclusion is: "Much ballyhooed back-to-the-city markets including Chicago, New York, Washington, DC, and San Francisco suffered double-digit percentage losses within the five-mile zone [of downtown]." Rather, the top metro areas gaining in boomer population are Las Vegas, Tampa–St. Petersburg, and Phoenix. In 2010, Kotkin chronicled his concerns about the "war on suburbia" being orchestrated in Washington, DC. Kotkin's defense of the suburbs is occasionally as hyperbolic as are the New Urbanists' anti-suburban diatribes. Still, his essential point is accurate: the single-family home remains the predominant choice of most Americans. The pattern is changing, however. The ever-larger home is no longer inevitable. Nor is the at-least-a-quarter-acre lot likely to be a standard for delivery of subdivisions. Houses and lots are shrinking to meet price points and lifestyle expectations. Phoenix is at the forefront of this trend, given its historic development of small lots and contained, walled backyards. Patio homes, attached townhomes, and condos will command a slowly increasing share of the new housing market in suburban cities.

Even if there were strong evidence that Americans were ending their centuries-long love affair with single-family homes, there are simply too many houses built since World War II to be abandoned. The number may approach 100 million.[40] Even for those who see the suburbanization of America as a mistake, the embedded materials, energy, and investment in so many houses deserve a measure of respect. It would be shockingly unsustainable to bulldoze huge swaths of the American urban fabric to start over again, wasting all those homes and all that history.

In 2012, in the wake of the real estate downturn, the Museum of Modern Art in Manhattan saw an opportunity and sponsored a group of architects and visionaries to think about "shifting suburbia." The goal was to enlist urban thinkers in examining how the single-family home fabric of the American suburb could be shifted into a more sustainable form in the future. The architectural concepts included densifying the suburbs by building large, multi-family villages out of shipping containers, which could be stacked and combined in various configurations; rebuilding factory buildings as housing complexes; and even putting large apartment buildings in the existing public streets between single-family homes.[41] The exercise was intriguing, if not really very productive. Putting buildings in place of streets is an unlikely evolution—there are pipes underneath all those streets. In any case, the far more likely transformation of suburban cities' housing stock is already under way.

Architecturally, the best thing about a detached home on an individual lot is its adaptability. For a multi-generational need, you can enclose a carport and convert it into a bedroom. The single-family home may be expanded into the backyard, or a separate detached garage and "granny flat" can be added. In a single-family neighborhood, choices of individual adaptability are possible that are simply not available in a multistory apartment building. Without having to move, a single family may survive through numerous generations by modification and adaptation. Throughout Phoenix, mid-century ranch houses are currently a hot commodity. Young singles and families seek out these modest production-built homes because they are solidly built, have plenty of room for expansion, and can be opened up internally for a more contemporary lifestyle.

As Kotkin put it in a different context: never bet against the single-family home.[42] New subdivisions are also adapting to changing trends. Lot sizes are getting smaller and housing products more creative. Several national homebuilders have introduced model homes expressly designed for multi-generational occupancy. Lennar calls their product "Nextgen," the "home within a home." In Chandler, Arizona, a model of this home was erected in the IKEA parking lot.

Newer subdivisions throughout the West are seeing an increasing variety of creative housing products being built in a patio-home, zero-lot-line, or planned-area-development-type configuration, with ever-smaller lots and more common-area open space. The creativity of developers and homebuilding companies to further explore

Figure 5.7. A fairly ordinary Phoenix ranch house with recent "cool" remodeling. (Photo by author)

Figure 5.8. Ralph Haver designed entire subdivisions of mid-century modern ranches, which are now highly prized in today's market. (Photo by author)

Figure 5.9. Lennar's "NextGen" model was built in an IKEA parking lot for market-ing purposes and torn down after approximately twelve months. (Photo by author)

alternatives to the conventional quarter-acre lot will continue to present consumers with a broader range of choices. As those choices are made, they will drive creativity in different directions in the future.

In Phoenix in the early 2000s, developers seized on new opportunities for greater density and began building mid- and high-rise condominiums. Immediate issues arose with construction defect litigation—which could be easily brought as a class action. An even bigger problem was the risk of missing the market with a complex of hundreds of units. Another great benefit of the single-family home became clear: it is scaleable. Build a few and see if they sell, make adjustments if necessary. Townhomes, patio homes, and lower-density condos are similarly more scalable than high-rise units.

Figures 5.10a and 5.10b. Townhomes in Tempe and stacked condos in downtown Phoenix. (Photos by author)

Not only housing needs to adapt to new realities. Retail is consistently the most dynamic and rapidly changing aspect of urban development. This will continue to be the case going into the future. The inexorable shift of a major portion of retail sales onto the Internet will dramatically alter the percentage of the built environment that needs to be dedicated to the sale of goods. For cities like Phoenix, this means that thousands of acres that have been devoted to retail shopping centers will need to be completely repositioned. This will be a painful transition in some places where shopping centers survive minimal occupancies, boarded-up stores, and a derelict, graffiti-riddled appearance. Yet in the scheme of repositioning the suburban city, this is not bad news. Shopping centers are, by their very nature, well located—that was the point. These are good locations for other uses as retail uses shrink.

The retail phenomenon of the "big box" may turn out to be one of the shortest-lived incarnations of shopping. From the 1980s forward, "category killers" and discount stores became the dominant shopping form, building ever-larger, windowless boxes. Their huge footprints and acres of bare asphalt parking lots dominate the suburban landscape. Not only did they rapidly kill each other off, but they lost customers as the Internet attracted more and more—and younger—shoppers for durable, fungible goods. Today in the Phoenix metropolitan area alone, 280 "boxes" over 10,000 square feet sit vacant—the highest number in the United States. They are unlikely to ever see retail uses again. Their sites will need to be rebuilt with higher-density housing, employment, and other uses. So far, potential redevelopment for higher-density housing has proven to be economically challenging. Phoenix rental rates are generally too low to amortize the acquisition, demolition, and redevelopment cost. Rents in Phoenix are just beginning to justify structured parking, which can boost densities enough to command higher land prices.

A recent phenomenon in suburban cities is the rise of urban "activity nodes" within neighborhoods. These are generally the result of repositioning an older declining shopping center or strip commercial area into new, locally based restaurant/bar/entertainment locations. Such individual activity nodes have been the result of creative, small-scale urban developers recognizing opportunities, and a broad-based public acceptance of the need for interesting and unique local dining experiences within walking distance of vital urban neighborhoods. These nodes initially began to appear in affluent neighborhoods and seemed to be built around coffee, Internet accessibility, and dog-friendly patios. Increasingly, even "transitional" neighborhoods are seeing local retail revitalization— often with a more ethnic flavor than was originally the case. Declining arterial streets in Phoenix are being repopulated with locally owned, largely Hispanic businesses. Though this may alarm some longtime residents, it is a positive trend.

All over suburban cities today, there is evidence of the continuing vitality and adaptability of the post–World War II American development pattern. Investment in well-located older single-family neighborhoods is on the rise. Even the proliferation of home-improvement programs on cable television is evidence of the interest of younger generations in fixing up and revitalizing suburban neighborhoods. Vacant sites and downtrodden shopping centers are being repositioned with higher-density, multi-family uses. Urban activity nodes are appearing throughout suburbia. The urban fabric of suburban cities shows every sign of adapting into the future.

Chapter 6

Jobs and the Economy of Cities in the Sand

T HERE IS A FATALISTIC VIEW THAT PHOENIX will crumble back into the desert landscape from which it arose, as in Richard Florida's March 2009 article, "How the Crash Will Reshape America." Criticizing "cities in the sand," Florida wrote:

> But in the heady days of the housing bubble, some Sun Belt cities—Phoenix and Las Vegas are the best examples—developed economies centered largely on real estate and construction. With sunny weather and plenty of flat, empty land, they got caught in a classic boom cycle. Although these places drew tourists, retirees, and some industry—firms seeking bigger footprints at lower costs—much of the cities' development came from, well, development itself.[1]

Given the economic downturn that occurred between 2005 and 2008, Florida's criticism clearly had resonance. Housing prices declined, and job creation nearly ceased. Then, in late 2011, housing sales and prices began to tick upward. In the first quarter of 2012, prices were increasing, at times by 50¢ to $1 per square foot per day. Home values overall rose about 25 percent from the trough. Job creation was slowly gaining.[2] It looked at that point as though production homebuilding was about to bounce back once again. But then things cooled. Like much of the United States, Phoenix has experienced a sputtering recovery.

Cities built on boosterism and real estate speculation are prone to boom-and-bust cycles even under the best of circumstances. Real estate development is a volatile and cyclical industry in which the laws of supply and demand operate with relentless force. For a place like Phoenix, built largely on the goal of importing residents from elsewhere with the promise of inexpensive housing and an attractive lifestyle, a boom-and-bust cycle is probably unavoidable. In the last part of the twentieth century and the beginning of the twenty-first, the economic policies of the federal government dramatically and repeatedly exacerbated boom and bust.

Phoenix has often been the last stop before some business operation moves offshore. The city has been a low-cost American environment for electronics manufacturing or call centers, for example. Both of those industries have represented booms in past job growth, but in both cases that employment base has eroded when it became clearly cheaper to build chips or answer phones in India or Malaysia than it was in Arizona.

It is accurate to see Phoenix as a place driven by development.[3] It is also fair to criticize an overreliance on construction and growth as leading to cyclical extremes. Nevertheless, development is not a single industry like automobiles or steel that can be ravaged by changing consumer patterns or global competition. Real estate is not portable—it is about accommodating demographic trends. An economy built on development is more diversified than it may seem, because people moving to a place bring with them capital investment, work effort, and entrepreneurial zeal. As a result, the non–real estate side of the Phoenix economy is well diversified. According to a 2012 report by Arizona State University's L. William Seidman Research Institute, the regional economy is driven by several sectors, including waste management, administrative support, finance and insurance, hospitality and restaurants, and high-tech manufacturing.[4]

The Urban Land Institute's *2013 Emerging Trends in Real Estate* uses Moody's Industrial Diversity Scale to rank America's largest cities for economic diversity. The nation as a whole is assigned a value of 1.0. Phoenix scores a .79, placing it ahead of Los Angeles, New York, Philadelphia, San Francisco, and Houston but behind Atlanta, Dallas, and Chicago.[5] This diversity is the result of a multitude of small businesses and no really dominant big business. The picture remains of a place with moderate incomes, a broad variety of jobs, and no clear economic identity beyond growth. Population increase has been the consistent measure of success for Phoenix's self-image. Given this reality, the nature of recent booms and busts is worth considering.

In hindsight, it seems ludicrous that anyone would suggest that the government should guarantee the economic performance of an industry that it does not regulate. Of course, that is precisely what the US Congress was persuaded to do in 1982. The federally insured mortgage and savings and loan associations had built postwar America. The inflation of the 1970s meant that the savings and loans were paying high interest rates on their deposits, and loaning it out for home mortgages was a money-losing proposition. So in the deregulatory ethic of the era, the solution was to allow the savings and loans to invest in a wider variety of businesses.

In the world of Arizona real estate, savings and loan deregulation meant direct investments in development projects. No one figured out the system better than Charlie Keating. Keating had first moved to Phoenix in 1978, when he bought Continental Homes and turned it into the largest homebuilder in the state. In 1983, he bought Lincoln Savings in California for $51 million and obtained a billion dollars' worth of investment leverage. While Charlie Keating was the most infamous player in the overheated market of the mid-1980s, virtually every savings and loan in Arizona was caught up in a frenzy of real estate investment. For a short time, it seemed that the new entrepreneurial options for publicly insured money were a stroke of extraordinary good fortune for the Sunbelt.[6]

In 1988, *Barron's* ran a legendary piece by Jonathan Laing entitled "Phoenix Descending: Is Boomtown U.S.A. Going Bust?" The article chronicled the savings and loan industry's diversification into real estate. It also noted the rise of home foreclosures, the mounting vacancies, and the downturn in migration, all of which pointed, in Laing's view, to a potential crash such as had been seen in other Western cities:

> In the end, Phoenix is proving to be as much a one-industry town as Houston or Denver, though the locals are only now waking up to that fact. The industry isn't oil, of course. It's growth. For if one totes up all the construction workers, real-estate brokers and syndicators, insurance salesmen, architects, appraisers, bankers and thrift operatives, and government employees directly involved in new construction, the number comes to nearly 20 percent of the work force.[7]

Laing proved prophetic. During the first half of 1989, banks in Arizona lost more money than those in any other state.[8] Keating's holding company, American Continental, filed for bankruptcy, and immediately thereafter the federal regulators seized Lincoln Savings—which became the biggest thrift failure in US history. By 1992, the federal government's Resolution Trust Corporation

(RTC) was the largest real estate player in Arizona. The bubble burst. Brokers who had been making hundreds of thousands of dollars a year found themselves selling cars, and real estate lawyers had to go back to litigation. The press and the elected officials quit worrying about quality of life and went back to yearning for the next boom. Their wish was quickly granted. The market crash began to turn around beginning in 1993. At first development came slowly, since this time it was driven by actual demand for houses and commercial space, instead of by money looking for a place to land. Even without the free-flowing lubrication of federally insured money, the boom that occurred in the national economy beginning in the mid-1990s energized Phoenix right back into a high-growth cycle. From a high of 21,432 single-family permits in the Phoenix metro area in 1988, the number had fallen by 50 percent to 12,950 in 1990. By 1996, the rebound was to 39,646, just short of an all-time high.[9]

At the dawn of the new millennium, things were looking good for metro Phoenix. The city seemed poised to become the great place it had always wanted to be. All the ingredients were coming together in support of a boom surpassing any in its prior history. About 40,000 new units (both single-family and multi-family) were being permitted in Maricopa County every year from 1998 through 2002. By 2003, the number was up to 46,000. In 2004 and 2005, the numbers hovered around 60,000 new units. In 2004, headlines in the local papers proclaimed that, based on census estimates, the city of Phoenix itself had passed Philadelphia in population to become the fifth-largest city in America.

Meanwhile, Phoenix continued to debate the merits of growth. In November 2000, the citizens of Arizona were called upon to vote on Proposition 202, the "Citizens Growth Management Initiative," a proposal by the Sierra Club and others to circumscribe cities and towns in Arizona with rigid growth boundaries. When they spoke at the polls, Arizona voters resoundingly defeated the growth boundary proposal. There were a number of reasons why that happened, not the least of which is that developer and home-builder groups spent nearly $5 million to defeat it. Another major factor in its defeat was that, as the campaign progressed, one out of every three or four vehicles in the Valley seemed to be a white pickup truck with a bumper sticker saying "No on 202, Your Job Depends On It." These trucks belonged to the contractors, subcontractors, and suppliers who fueled the metro area's economy.[10]

The formula for the enormous boom early in the new century included familiar ingredients: sunshine, infrastructure, inexpensive land on the edge of town, efficient homebuilding, and more freeways. In addition, several of the large, independent communities surrounding the city of Phoenix sought to create distinctive niches. Scottsdale was really hitting its stride as a major tourist destination, with ever-larger and fancier hotels and a number of high-end, golf-course-oriented, master-planned communities. These attracted c-suite corporate officers to second homes, some of whom liked it enough to move their businesses, and the area around Scottsdale's airport became a major job center.

In the East Valley, meanwhile, Mesa and Chandler were exploding. Mesa's population in 2000 made it the forty-second-largest city in the United States. By 2005, the population of the city of Mesa exceeded that of Miami, Atlanta, or Minneapolis. Job growth was on a parallel track. Metro Phoenix in the early 2000s was consistently appearing in the top ten metro areas in the country for job growth. Some of the jobs continued to be related to high-tech manufacturing, though most microchip production was moving offshore. Rather, Phoenix became a major location for call centers. USAA, the giant insurance company focused on serving the military and based in San Antonio, wanted a presence farther to the west in order to serve the needs of customers calling in from the West Coast and the Pacific Rim. They started scouting the Phoenix area in the late 1990s and chose a location on the north Black Canyon Freeway, which opened in 2001. The facility quickly grew to several thousand employees.

In addition to the success of the traditional formula for a Sunbelt city, there were signs in the early 2000s that the metropolitan Phoenix market was beginning to mature, and some deliberate efforts to diversify the economic base took root. In 2002, following a major push by the business community to build a bioscience base, the Translational Genomics Institute opened in downtown Phoenix as the first piece of an emerging medical complex that would eventually include a branch of the University of Arizona's College of Medicine.

Probably the most consequential event of the early 2000s was the dramatic expansion of Arizona State University after the arrival in 2002 of a new president, Michael Crow. An aggressive, visionary leader, he rebranded ASU as the "new American university" and sought to dramatically expand it both in size and quality. The opening of ASU's downtown campus coincided with the arrival of the light-rail connection between downtown and Tempe, providing a remarkable synergy.

Two of the Valley cities sought to take deliberate transformative action to distinguish their community from the seamless proliferation of beige stucco houses and shopping centers. Tempe, which had become "landlocked" (unable to annex more territory) in the 1970s, sought to refocus itself as an increasingly urban college town with a major urban amenity: the Tempe Town Lake.[11] The Town Lake had been dreamed of since 1966, when an ASU architecture class envisioned revitalizing the dry Salt River bed as a major urban amenity. The vision of the riverbed once again becoming a water feature and center of urban life was nurtured by Tempe mayors Harry Mitchell and Neil Giuliano as well as city council and staff members for decades. It finally came to fruition in the summer of 1999. Though the lake was roundly criticized as a "waste of water" by some observers, it was quickly embraced by a population seeking an urban gathering spot for sporting events, festivals, and simply the kind of passive "hanging out" that takes place in big cities but that the Phoenix area had often lacked. The City of Tempe

Figure 6.1. Tempe Town Lake near Arizona State University and the Mill Avenue District, with new office and residential development spurred by the lake. (© Shutterstock: Jeffrey Rasmussen)

envisioned it not simply as a visual and recreational amenity but as an attractor for major office buildings and employers. The first of a series of high-rises located on the shore of the Tempe Town Lake and burdened with a special tax assessment to pay for lake operation opened in early 2002.

Meanwhile, Glendale, the oldest and largest of the separate west-side municipalities, set out on a separate course to transform itself into something beyond a bedroom suburb, using the tool of professional sports. The metro area had landed a National Hockey League franchise named the Arizona Coyotes in 1996. Initially, the team shared the downtown arena (then called America West) with the Phoenix Suns of the National Basketball Association. This was not a satisfactory arrangement, and after a failed proposal in Scottsdale, Glendale launched an aggressive bid to court the Coyotes for a new west-side arena that would become the anchor of a shopping and entertainment district. The arena opened in 2003.

Similarly, the Arizona Cardinals football team had been playing in ASU's Sun Devil Stadium in Tempe since their arrival in the state in 1988. This arrangement also did not work, and the Cardinals had long been seeking a climate-controlled stadium where daytime pro football games could be more tolerable. Various locations in downtown Phoenix or near the airport had been considered, but in 2000 the state Tourism and Sports Authority, which had been created precisely to build a stadium for the Cardinals, selected a site in Glendale near the existing hockey arena. The stadium opened in 2006. Together, the Cardinal's stadium and the Coyotes' facility were designed to transform the western edge of the city of Glendale into a vibrant, intense, mixed-use entertainment district.

Glendale's transformational strategy proved problematic. The promised commercial and residential community that was to grow up around the sports venues was hit especially hard by the economic downturn that began in 2007, and it failed to deliver either the development or the expected tax revenue that the city had sought. Further, as things began to unfold, it became clear that the expected revenue from the hockey arena was far less than had been projected. Glendale voters expressed unhappiness with their city's growth and investment strategy, and they elected a set of new council members who were much less enthused with the city's attempted transformation.[12]

As early as 2006, there were clear signs that the booming growth of metropolitan Phoenix was again cruising for a crash. The sudden increase in homebuilding from 30,000–40,000 houses per year to more than 60,000 was not the result of some tectonic economic shift in the attractiveness of Arizona as a place. Rather, like the boom that had resulted from the deregulation of savings and loans in the 1990s, it was the result of creative financial wizardry.

For generations, the American home mortgage loan had been one of the safest possible financial investments. Default rates were low and the value of the underlying security, the single-family home, seemed to always go up. So what could be better than to

Figure 6.2. Glendale, Arizona, sports and mixed-use venues from above. (© Shutterstock: Tim Roberts Photography)

package home mortgages into pools of financial obligations and sell them to investors? These capitalized pools, known as "collateralized mortgage-backed securities" or "CMBS," proved so popular in the marketplace that they actually drove demand for more home mortgages than the normal market could produce. As a result, subprime mortgages—loans to high-risk homebuyers—began rapidly proliferating in the early 2000s. Many of the pools included large numbers of these subprime loans. The theory was that the unlikelihood of a high percentage of such loans defaulting all at once would protect the pools against significant risk. In fact, as it soon became clear, the whole scheme was just one more ploy to privatize gains and socialize losses.

The ready availability of subprime mortgages meant that suddenly there were vast numbers of new homebuyers entering the market. For a place like Phoenix that thrived on efficient home construction and moderately priced housing, many of these buyers were being pulled out of the rental housing market into houses they could not really afford. In addition, large numbers of new homes were being acquired primarily as investments with the expectation of continued price escalation. Between May 2002 and May 2006, the median price of a home in Phoenix rose by 85 percent.[13]

Meanwhile, as detailed by author Michael Lewis in *The Big Short*, beginning in about 2003 other investors began buying a derivative called a credit default swap.[14] These speculators were betting that mortgage defaults would occur. Conversely the sellers of such investments, such as insurance giant AIG, bet that they would not. A virtually unlimited amount could be wagered in this market on the same set of securities. When massive defaults did begin to occur, the companies that had been selling default swap obligations were unable to meet their financial and legal obligations, thereby compounding the impact of the defaults.

Metropolitan Phoenix felt the effects of this collapse as dramatically as anywhere in the country. From 2005 to 2010, the price of homes in metro Phoenix fell by almost 50 percent. Arizona as a state went from creating 121,000 jobs between October 2005 and October 2006 to losing 183,000 jobs in 2009. From nearly 60,000 new homes built in Maricopa County in 2005, the number dropped to 40,000 in 2006, 30,000 in 2007, then plummeted to 13,000 in 2008, fewer than 8,500 in 2009, 7,000 in 2010, and only 6,000 in 2011. It was the biggest bust ever in a place with a long history of boom and bust.

The Great Recession revealed the overreliance of a Sunbelt boomtown on construction activity as the source of economic growth. In Phoenix, nearly 36 percent of growth in the economy between 2002 and 2006 was based on real estate and construction. By contrast, in Dallas–Fort Worth only 18 percent of the economy was tied to those industries, and in Charlotte, North Carolina, it was only 15 percent.[15] So when the recession hit, Charlotte's job losses, though severe, had only resulted in home prices dropping by 11 percent from peak versus 50 percent in Phoenix. Phoenix and Las Vegas saw the highest percentages of houses go into foreclosure of any cities

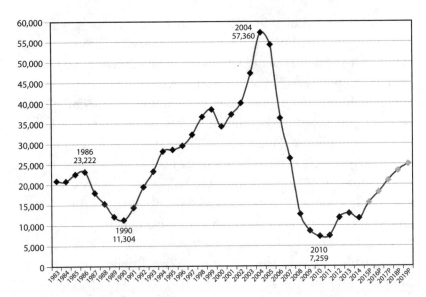

Figure 6.3. *Single-family homebuilding permits track the boom and bust of metro Phoenix. (Source: Historical permit data based upon US Census Bureau data. Permit projections provided by Belfiore Real Estate Consulting.)*

in the country. In Phoenix, more than one in seventeen households received a foreclosure filing; in Las Vegas, it was one in eleven.

The doomsayers decrying the unsustainability of Sunbelt growth cities began piling on. Richard Florida's critique in the *Atlantic Monthly* in 2009 was followed by Justin Hollander, who, in his book *Sunburnt Cities*, wrote that Sunbelt cities should learn from Detroit and plan for their depopulation.[16]

Every time there is a bust in the economy, there emerges a deep-seated insecurity in a city of newcomers, transplants, and transients. Innumerable public events, forums, and gatherings are held questioning how to diversify the economy of a place that is hurting from the overreliance on real estate.

Growth may be the activity most basic to the self-image of a place like Phoenix, but simultaneously it is also the activity most threatening: both its *raison d'être* and its curse. The negative impact of the Great Recession of the early twenty-first century is still being felt. Unlike the real estate collapse of the 1990s, this time the city did not snap back quickly. Indeed, the recovery lag in Phoenix and Las Vegas is worse than in most other places.

Nevertheless, Hollander's prediction in *Sunburnt Cities* that cities like Phoenix and Las Vegas would suffer a dramatic erosion in population has not, so far, come true. The analogy to the hollowing out of Detroit is not apropos. Detroit's long and steady decline resulted from its reliance on one massive industrial base for its employment, and as that industry, automobile manufacturing, shifted, changed, and moved away, the city slowly declined. Phoenix, on the other hand, saw the Great Recession increase the amplitude of boom and bust that it had experienced throughout its life. While the recovery has continued to lag, it may be that a slower recovery, based less on a booming homebuilding market and more on slow and steady job growth, will ultimately prove to be more sustainable.

The sentiment that there should be a conscious effort to smooth out the boom-and-bust nature of the economy and to decrease an overreliance on real estate is repeatedly expressed by people from all quarters of Phoenix's economy, even including those who work in the real estate industry. In May 2015, for example, John Graham, a highly respected Phoenix developer and chairman of a new organization called Velocity, expressed a concern that without a new business plan, the Phoenix metropolitan area might remain stuck in repetitive business cycles yielding low-wage jobs and a second-tier economic status. "The status quo is not an option," said Graham.[17] Hiring a consulting firm from out of town to think about improving Phoenix's economy is a repeated theme of insecurity. At various times, the Battelle Institute, SRI, and others have all taken a look at how to diversify the Phoenix economy. The new Velocity effort is driven by the Greater Phoenix Economic Council, the economic development association of Valley cities and businesses, with consulting work by the Brookings Institution's Metropolitan Policy Program. The effort contains a more detailed and specific business plan for the urban area than has been the case in most of the past studies. The effort is intended to focus on export growth, advanced industries, and the creation of an "innovation economy."

Most aspirational-type cities across the United States have engaged in similar introspective efforts to think about how to make themselves more like Silicon Valley. Richard Florida's *The Rise of the Creative Class*, published in 2002, caused many cities to think differently about the components of business attraction.[18] Florida urged cities to focus not simply on low taxes or economic incentives but rather on a broader suite of "coolness" factors that make a city more livable and more interesting. His thesis was that in the emerging urban growth of America, economic success for metropolitan areas will be driven not so much by employers deciding where to build as by millennials deciding where to live and businesses following them. Whether he is right or not is still a hotly debated topic. In Phoenix, Robert Robb, the *Arizona Republic's* widely respected editorial columnist, has been a consistent critic of the chase for urban "creative class" workers, terming it the "Peter Pan theory of millennials"—meaning that it is unrealistic to think that they will "never grow up, marry, have kids, want those kids to have a lawn to play on, or want to put their kids in higher-performing suburban schools."[19]

In 2012, economist Enrico Moretti returned to the "creative class" issue with *The New Geography of Jobs*.[20] Moretti begins his dialogue by looking at two California cities, Menlo Park and Visalia, which in 1969 had relatively similar demographics. Menlo Park was a broadly diversified but still largely working-class community in the Bay Area. Visalia, though less well educated, was not dramatically different. Moretti tells the story of an engineer relocating from Menlo Park to Visalia because housing was less expensive, and he sought a similar but less hectic lifestyle. It turned out to be a bad choice. In the period since then, the two cities have moved far apart. Menlo Park is now deeply embedded in the economy of the Silicon

Valley as a place of highly educated, high-wage knowledge workers. Visalia, meanwhile, has skidded down the economic scale with almost no change in the percentage of workers with a college degree and an increasingly isolated agricultural and blue-collar economy. Morretti's point is that cities are increasingly sorting into "winners" and "losers" based on their participation in the innovation economy.

For an insecure but large metropolitan area like Phoenix, Moretti's view of American cities being divided into the high-education/ high-wage "haves" and low-education/low-wage "have-nots" is a cautionary and alarming tale. From 1960 through 1980, Arizona exceeded the US average in the percentage of its population with bachelor's degrees. From 1990 to 2010, Phoenix's percentage fell behind. The city has often lagged behind the national average in per capita income, but in 1970 through 2000 Phoenix drew relatively close. As of 2013, the city was $6,000 behind the US per capita average income. There are a number of reasons for this: a higher proportion of foreign immigrants, particularly from south of the border; a younger population; the loss of relatively high-paying construction jobs; and a high proportion of relatively low-wage retail and service industry jobs.

Velocity's solutions to this problem have not yet fully emerged but are largely based around the need to increase investments in the educational system. Its immediate focus has been to try to spur greater investment in STEM (science, technology, engineering, and math) education at the community college and university level. In the Great Recession, Arizona put a tighter squeeze on university budgets than any other state. In 2015, the state was spending 47 percent less per college student than in 2008.[21] Arizona State University creatively found ways to survive huge cuts in state funding, through tuition and fee increases and increased research grants. Universities have flexibility in revenue sources that are not available in the K–12 system, however.

The most serious consequence of the Great Recession for Arizona was the dramatic decline in spending on K–12 education. Any

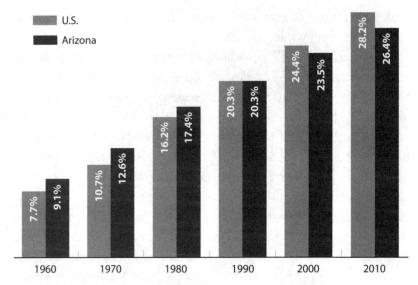

Figure 6.4. Bachelor's degrees as a percentage of total population shows Arizona falling behind.

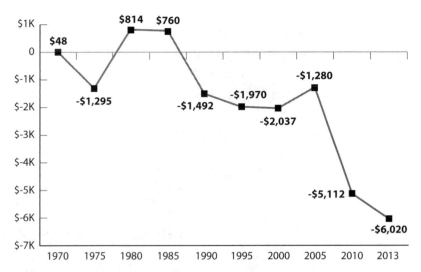

Figure 6.5. The difference between Phoenix and US average per capita income, 1970–2013. (Source: Bureau of Economic Analysis, US Bureau of Labor Statistics)

scheme to diversify the economy and create higher-wage employment is severely undermined by an underperforming educational system. Arizona's conservative legislature has long seemed to have the attitude that the educational bureaucracy is excessively bloated and unreasonably expensive, and that it should be cut along with the rest of state government. On a per capita basis, the state of Arizona has cut its state budget significantly since 1990. In 1990, the state took in about $50 for every $1,000 of personal income in the state. By 2013, this number was down to $38. Over the same period, as a result of decreases in state taxes the proportion of the state budget devoted to education declined, down 21 percent since 1990. The consequence of all this is that, by 2013, Arizona was dead last among American states in classroom spending per pupil. Arizona's position in education spending has been near the bottom for so long that the public seems to have quit listening to the essentially circular argument that "we need to spend more on education because we do not spend enough on education."

In terms of teacher salaries in Phoenix versus teacher salaries in other cities with which Phoenix would like to compete, the

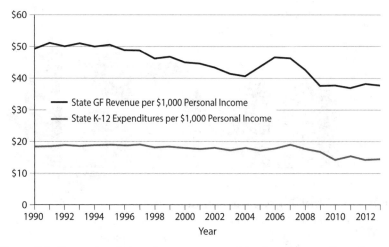

Figure 6.6. Comparing Arizona's tax revenues with education spending. (Source: Joint Legislative Budget Committee, Bureau of Economic Analysis)

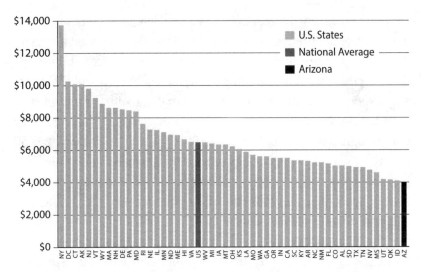

Figure 6.7. State per capita classroom expenditures. Arizona is dead last. (Source: Joint Legislative Budget Committee, Bureau of Economic Analysis)

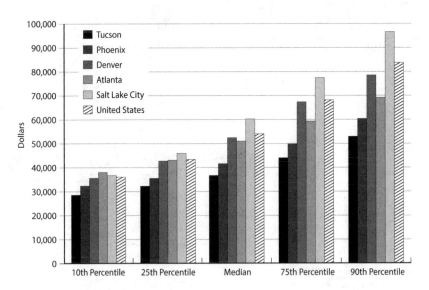

Figure 6.8. Elementary school teacher wages (adjusted for local cost of living). Eighty percent of all K–12 spending goes to salaries and benefits, so low education funding means low pay for teachers. Phoenix and Tucson teachers are paid substantially less than those in competitor cities, even when adjusted for cost of living.

difference is stark. Phoenix and Tucson rank near the bottom in teacher salaries of all the commonly viewed competitive cities.

One of the emerging strategies to improve urban Arizona's economy focuses on the relationship between Phoenix and Tucson as one of the nation's emerging megapolitan regions.

The differences between Phoenix and Tucson are remarkably pronounced for places that lie less than 100 miles apart and are connected by a single freeway and a really boring drive. For generations, the two cities have followed dramatically different growth trajectories. The shorthand view of metropolitan Phoenix is that it is a land of unconstrained growth where developers rule and 100,000 newcomers a year are embraced and assimilated. Houses surrounded by lawns and leafy trees and golf courses spring up in place of plowed fields or creosote desert. Houses covered with peel-and-stick cultured stone announce the latest master-planned community with a name manufactured, seemingly, in Esperanto.

To the south, Tucson is thought to represent a different place: slower, smaller, where people try to live *in* the desert instead of *near* the desert. Houses look plainer, with more flat roofs, and there is not a lot of grass. The place is dustier and scruffier, in part because there are few sidewalks. Arterial streets bustle with cars and trucks because freeways would spoil the small-city ambiance.

The conceit is too simplistic. It is inaccurate to portray Maricopa County (Phoenix) as an unplanned hodgepodge of sprawl designed only to consume the desert. The area's quality of life is better than that. Pima County (Tucson) is not really a collection of environmentally sensitive flower children living in harmony with their surroundings; its infrastructure is often overwhelmed and its economy

Table 6.1. Phoenix and Tucson Population Growth and Expansion Comparison

	1890	1910	1930	1940	1960	1980
Phoenix	3,152	11,134	48,118	65,414	439,170	789,704
Tucson	5,150	13,193	32,506	36,818	212,892	330,537

Source: US Census Bureau.

is slow to create quality jobs. Different attitudes and histories of the neighboring counties provide lessons for the growth trajectory of suburban cities. The stories of Pima and Maricopa Counties are driven by the sagas of Tucson and Phoenix. As chronicled by Michael Logan in *Desert Cities*, the two cities grew somewhat in parallel from the 1890s through the 1920s. By the end of the 1920s, though, Roosevelt Dam had secured for Phoenix the unbeatable advantage of a major stable water supply. Phoenix fared much better during the Great Depression, and thereafter the cities' attitudes toward growth and development began to diverge.[22] The raw numbers in Table 6.1 tell a story.

Agriculture and abundant water gave Maricopa County the opportunity to market a lifestyle of sunshine, citrus trees, and grass—a lower-budget alternative to Southern California that could intercept nomads from Ohio, who had intended to go to Los Angeles but ran out of gas. Pima County was not on the same migratory path, and instead it much more consciously sold an "Old West" lifestyle of self-reliance and dusty streets. Tucson's cowboy image attracted new citizens with a libertarian bent who saw city government more negatively than did new Maricopa County residents.

Despite their divergent histories, at least since the 1960s, there was a vague expectation that Phoenix and Tucson would somehow one day merge into one continuous urbanized area. No such prediction has quite come true. In fact, the area between Tucson and

Phoenix has a number of constraints—most visibly, an Indian reservation—that make continued urbanization without any breaks an unlikely scenario. In the early 2000s, Arthur C. Nelson and Robert E. Lang, then both at Virginia Tech, evolved a more sophisticated way of thinking about the ever-larger urban agglomerations that were arising in the United States. Their work, most extensively chronicled in the book *Megapolitan America*, recognized that certain metropolitan areas in the United States were merging into one another.[23] Their methodology for determining such mergers was based on commuting patterns overlapping to the extent that an "employment interchange factor" indicated a merger of economic units. Nelson and Lang recognized Arizona's Sun Corridor as one of these emerging megapolitan regions.

A few of the hallmarks of the Sun Corridor suggest challenges and opportunities for sustaining its economy.[24] Though the area covered by the Sun Corridor is geographically large (and somewhat challenging to define), one of its distinguishing characteristics is how much open space exists and will continue to exist by virtue of protected land. Beyond the protected open space, there are also hundreds of square miles of State Trust land. This land is not protected, but rather is owned by the state for the purpose of making money for Arizona's schools. Through various mechanisms it can ultimately be released for development. The most prominent piece of land is referred to as Superstition Vistas and represents a 275-square-mile area lying in the East Valley that could one day be home to hundreds of thousands of additional residents.[25]

The fact that the Sun Corridor will include thousands of acres of open space creates an urban development opportunity for better thinking about natural area open space and its relationship to urban development. While the State Trust land is presumably developable, it is intermingled with challenging topographies and is adjacent to long-term undevelopable open space. The development of this property is designed to help fund education in Arizona over the long term but could also serve as a laboratory for development innovation. That the State Trust land exists in large blocks frees it up from many of the traditional constraints of development.

Unfortunately for this potential vision of sensitive development, it is also true that that hundreds of thousands of lots within the Sun Corridor were "entitled" in the boom times of the early 2000s. After the downturn occurred, these lots remained on the books with a "property right" to development. Arizona's unique Proposition 207 makes it almost impossible to roll back these development approvals, greatly constraining the ability of cities to regulate the future growth of the Sun Corridor.[26] Prop 207 was adopted by Arizona voters in 2006 and is an attempt to require compensation for any new land-use laws that constrain the uses of property. This will mean that many of the people who are owners of the entitled lots in the Sun Corridor will threaten lawsuits for tens of millions of dollars in damages if the entitlements of those lots are changed.

The challenges and opportunity of changing demographics in America are dramatically displayed in the Tables 6.2 and 6.3. It is not just the Sun Corridor where the minority nonwhite share of the population is going to dramatically increase—it is the entire United States. In New York–Philadelphia and the Steel Corridor (Pittsburgh), the minority share of growth actually exceeds the overall population growth of the entire region. This is because the non-minority share of the population in those two megapolitans continues to grow even as total population is declining.

There is another demographic misconception of the Sun Corridor: that its population growth is disproportionately made up of retirees. In fact, the senior component of the population of the Sun Corridor in 2010–2040 is only about 31 percent, lower than that of Puget Sound, Atlanta, Southern California, or Las Vegas. Here again, the most interesting comparison is to the Steel Corridor or New England, where even with a declining overall population the number of seniors is dramatically increasing.

Demographically, the picture of the Sun Corridor that emerges is that by 2040 it will be the largest urban area west of the Mississippi

Table 6.2. White and Minority Share of Population Change by Megapolitan Area, 2010–2040 (in thousands)

Megapolitan Area	Population Change	White Non-Hispanic Population Change	Minority Population Change	Minority Share of Growth (%)
Puget Sound	1,811	127	1,685 (6)	97.0 (3)
Willamette	1,389	208	1,181 (8)	85.0 (4)
Southern California	7,636	(2,358)	9,994 (1)	130.9 (1)
Las Vegas	1,673	541	1,132 (9)	67.7 (9)
Sun Corridor	3,436	845	2,591 (5)	75.4 (7)
Front Range	2,021	516	1,505 (7)	74.5 (8)
Dallas–Fort Worth	3,684	827	2,857 (3)	77.6 (6)
Houston	3,284	(64)	3,348 (2)	102.0 (2)
Atlanta	3,679	963	2,716 (4)	77.8 (5)
Steel Corridor	163	(438)	601	368.1
New York–Philadelphia	6,053	(3,376)	9,430	155.8

Source: Arthur C. Nelson and Robert E. Lang, *Megapolitan America: A New Vision for Understanding America's Metropolitan Geography*, Table 7.6 (Chicago: APA Planners Press, 2011), 70.

Table 6.3. Megapolitan Area Senior Population Change and Share of Total Population Change, 2010–2040 (in thousands)

Megapolitan Area	Total Population Change 2010–2040	Senior Population Change 2010–2040	Seniors as Share of Population Change 2010–2040 (%)
Puget Sound	1,811	710 (6)	39.2 (2)
Willamette	1,389	448 (9)	32.3 (4)
Southern California	7,636	3,558 (1)	46.6 (1)
Las Vegas	1,673	557 (7)	37.3 (3)
Sun Corridor	3,436	1,090 (4)	31.7 (5)
Front Range	2,021	546 (8)	27.0 (9)
Dallas–Fort Worth	3,684	1,094 (3)	29.7 (8)
Houston	3,284	998 (5)	30.4 (7)
Atlanta	3,679	1,143 (2)	31.1 (6)
Steel Corridor	163	703	430.6
New England	1,675	1,151	68.8

Source: Arthur C. Nelson and Robert E. Lang, *Megapolitan America: A New Vision for Understanding America's Metropolitan Geography*, Table 7.12 (Chicago: APA Planners Press, 2011), 76.

not located in either Texas or California. It will be denser, younger, and more Hispanic than most other megapolitan areas. And, in reaching that position between 2010 and 2040, it will be the fastest growing of America's large megapolitan areas.

People in metropolitan Phoenix and Tucson are still struggling to figure out what the Sun Corridor means to the future of each place. For Tucson, the primary benefit of megapolitan thinking is that being part of the Sun Corridor elevates their city to a competitive economic plateau very unlike where they stand on their own. Instead of viewing metropolitan peers as Albuquerque or Tulsa, by being part of the Sun Corridor Tucson becomes part of an urban area that can compete with Atlanta, Denver, or Seattle. To businesspeople in Tucson, this is an obvious advantage. To those who are steeped in traditional Tucsonans' negative view of Phoenix, the benefit is less clear. While most Phoenicians are generally inclined to ignore Tucson, there are at least three significant advantages to megapolitan-type thinking for Phoenix.

First, the border with Mexico will become an increasingly important economic driver. Mexico is already Arizona's number-one trading partner by far. For a long time, Phoenix simply did not pay much attention to the border. It was far away and a place to visit to buy trinkets and eat street food. When Phoenix finally did wake up to its proximity to the border, it did so with a vengeance, concluding that illegal aliens were the source of most of the state's problems, and both the border and anyone who crossed it needed to be demonized. Senate Bill 1070 and the antics of Sheriff Joe Arpaio in Maricopa County were nationally visible manifestations of knee-jerk hostility that hurt the region's economy. This incredibly counterproductive instinct stands in stark contrast to Tucson, which has had a much more sophisticated and subtle understanding of the relationship with Mexico. Sun Corridor–wide thinking should move toward the Tucsonan view and realize that the border is a huge benefit to the state.

Second, the University of Arizona, as the senior research university in the state, remains an important and driving presence of the state's economy. The U of A has a national prominence in optics, aerospace, hydrology, and a number of other critical areas. Most significantly for Phoenix, the presence of the U of A medical school, which opened in 2006, is part of the transformation of downtown Phoenix from a ghetto of bureaucrats and lawyers to a much more vital urban center.

Third, there is a risk in the embrace of megapolitan growth that the ever-larger urban concentrations will simply become a seam-less web of beige stucco houses and big-box shopping centers. The megapolitan reality does not have to doom the distinctiveness of place in America. Rather, the sheer size of large urban areas today should underline the need for distinctive places. Tucson has been better than Phoenix at staking out an interesting self-image. Cit-ies like Portland and Austin have been especially skilled at devel-oping and then marketing their quirkiness to a restless millennial population. Tucson has a similar funky image but with a traditional desert Southwestern flavor. To compete in an increasingly diverse, competitive, and global environment, Phoenix could use a dose of Tucson's distinctive quirkiness.

The first version of Arizona as a place, "Arizona 1.0," was about mining copper and moving enough water to grow crops in a sunny environment. The next version, "Arizona 2.0," was about sunshine and cheap houses. Phoenix became a real city in that era, based on the desert becoming habitable and people from the Midwest want-ing to live in the sun. So for most of its life, Phoenix's aspiration as a city has been pretty simple: to get big. The formula worked, and now Phoenix is, by any measure, a large, robust, and relatively diversified urban area.

Despite the hand-wringing over the boom-and-bust nature of a city in the sand, the reality today is that even after the Great Recession, Phoenix maintains a significant measure of success among America's big cities (see table 6.4). Metropolitan Phoenix

Table 6.4. Number of Jobs Added, 1990–2011

Dallas	1,001,905	San Diego	242,656
Houston	897,016	Boston	208,340
Phoenix	*693,934*	Sacramento	196,164
Atlanta	689,720	Philadelphia	186,905
Miami	498,674	Kansas City	179,458
Riverside	436,935	Cincinnati	136,247
New York	432,677	Baltimore	127,648
Seattle	388,299	Pittsburgh	99,438
Orlando	387,112	St. Louis	79,130
Denver	384,041	San Francisco	58,349
Minneapolis	357,200	Cleveland	−48,811
San Antonio	328,996	Detroit	−150,269
Chicago	305,800	Los Angeles	−254,514
Portland	287,897		
Charlotte	256,933		
Tampa	252,145		

Source: Bureau of Economic Analysis, as of June 21, 2013.

started regaining jobs in the summer of 2010 and has since added 263,000, ranking eighth among big cities in the United States. Between 1990 and 2011, Phoenix was third highest among big cities in the United States in the number of jobs added, trailing only Dallas and Houston. Over that same period, the metro area added almost 700,000 jobs, more than the creative-class darlings of Seattle and Portland combined. These statistics demonstrate the magnitude of success embodied in the formula of sunshine, low taxes, and low cost of living.

Things will change in the future. The size of Phoenix today is such that growth rates will necessarily decline as a percentage of population base. Further, metropolitan Phoenix's maturing economy is evolving in a complex era in which business is becoming increasingly global, competition is growing increasingly fierce, and transformation is happening ever more quickly.

Elements of a continuingly diverse but maturing economy are apparent. State Farm's decision to locate one of its huge regional headquarters on the shore of the Tempe Town Lake was driven by access to a large and relatively low-cost workforce as well as the absence of natural disasters. The people who answer phones for an insurance company need to be located in a place where disaster is an uncommon event. Phoenix is free from hurricanes, earthquakes, and tornadoes. A flood in Arizona means there is water in the river-bed, or maybe in the streets, for a couple of hours. Forest fires are located outside of the city, far to the north. And the widely publicized haboob has little lingering negative effect. The power grid in Phoenix is more reliable than places that are subject to ice storms and have above-ground distribution lines. These assets make the central Arizona desert a good place to locate businesses that put a premium on reliability. Proximity to the Mexican border may one day become a huge benefit for the economy. The availability of large amounts of raw land for growth will continue to keep housing costs down.

These attributes form a suite of natural advantages for sustaining an economy in metropolitan Phoenix and the Sun Corridor. The question of whether the existence of these advantages is enough to sustain the economy of central Arizona, or whether government should have a role in trying to advance economic maturation and transformation, is especially complex in a place with libertarian instincts. So the final question about the sustainability of Phoenix must concern the role of government—that is, the role of politics.

Chapter 7

Politics, Resilience, and Survival

J UST AS THE *Death and Life of Great American Cities* offers seminal insights into the evolutionary growth and vitality of cities, so Jared Diamond's book *Collapse* illuminates why various societies have failed in human history. Diamond catalogs the factors that can stress a society to the point of extinction: (1) relationships with trading partners go awry, (2) the society is beset by enemies, (3) climate changes threaten a particular locale, (4) local resources are depleted beyond the point of sustainability, and (5) a place fails to respond adequately to the other four factors.[1] The most critical factor is the last. In the history of Phoenix, the Hohokam apparently failed to adapt to the challenges they faced.

This fifth factor is the question of resilience. It is the question of how flexible a society's decision-making structure is, how quickly it can react to a challenge, and whether it has the capacity to recognize a mistake and change course. Resilience is all about politics.

Many of America's suburban cities are in the southern half of the country—the Sunbelt region. They tend to be hot, and many of them are not located on a coast. Their politics lean toward the conservative. The reason for the conservative bent of suburban cities is complex. In part, it is the product of the mythology of the West as a place of rugged individualists. In part, it is the result of the area having been populated by people fleeing older cities, which they perceived as being "high tax" environments or being dominated by corrupt political machines. Ironically, in the West the perception of less need for an activist local government is often the result of an umbrella of federal protections and interventions in the economy. Vast tracts of federal land, the exploitation of federally owned natural resources, and massive investments by the federal government in airports, interstate highways, and water systems all made the urban West possible. Those massive investments made locally driven government seem less necessary. At the same time, those massive federal investments, and particularly the pattern of federal ownership, made Westerners resent their Big Brother on the East Coast dictating how things should be done.

The mix of "Sunbelt capitalism" (to use Elizabeth Tandy Shermer's phrase) is nowhere more evident than in Phoenix.[2] It was Phoenix, after all, that gave Barry Goldwater to the modern conservative movement. In recent years, the nonpartisan city council governments of metro Phoenix (including the City of Phoenix itself) have by and large been practical, efficient, and relatively pragmatic. Most philosophical differences have been compromised and managed, even in times of severe budget stress.

At the state level, however, Arizona has been consumed by political posturing and right-wing legislation like the infamous SB 1070, an attempt to make immigration a state issue. This disconnect comes from the excessive partisan divide that plagues all American politics today, but in Arizona's case it is further reinforced by term limits and public funding of elections. These two reforms have had the unintended consequences of facilitating fringe candidates, eroding institutional memory, and diminishing the influence of the business sector.

Arizona's demographics alone facilitate a political disconnect: Arizona has lots of old white people and lots of young minorities. William Frey of the Brookings Institution calculates the state's "cultural generation gap"—the white share of over-65s minus the white share of under-18s—at 41 percent, higher than that of any other state.[3]

Arizona's statewide elections are caught in a distillation loop. In 2012, about 35 percent of the electorate were registered Republicans, 30 percent were Democrats, and 33 percent were independent or "other." The non-party-affiliated component is the fastest growing, especially among younger citizens. There are significant barriers to the participation of such independents. The parties select their candidates in partisan primaries funded by the state. Increasingly, in this very red state, the Republican primary decides who will ultimately be elected. Only about 25 percent of registered Republican voters participate in the primary. This means that 25 percent of 35 percent of registered voters are ultimately deciding who is elected to statewide office—resulting in about 8 percent of registered voters making that choice. Since only about two-thirds of the voting-age population is even registered to vote, this means that about 5 percent of those who could participate are actually making meaningful voting decisions.

The result is that statewide offices in Arizona are relatively easily captured by zealous partisan conservatives. As an increasing number of voters are turned off by this result, more and more leave the two parties to become independents, further distilling the small piece of the electorate that is actually deciding. This has driven the elected representatives in the state legislature further and further to the right, even as the overall population has grown and moderated. It is not surprising that "The Arizona We Want" poll conducted by

Gallup in 2009 found that only 10 percent of Arizonans believe that elected officials represent their interests.[4]

How Arizona got to its particular political perspective is worth analyzing in light of the fate of suburban cities. Arizona is often the butt of political jokes nationally, as well as occasional analysis about the prevalence of "tea party" attitudes in the Sonoran Desert. Ken Silverstein in 2010 wrote an article in *Harper's* magazine called "Tea Party in the Sonora."[5] His conclusion: a "confluence of nativism and antigovernment sentiment makes Arizona fertile ground for an especially showy brand of symbolic politics." Arizona, he suggested, was a harbinger of the future of conservative American politics. From the early stages of the 2016 presidential race, this cautionary note appears prophetic.

Arizona's politics are a mix of factors, which are present in different proportions in other suburban cities. First in Arizona is the *geography of insecurity*. The principal city, after all, is named after a bird that burns itself up. This is not an image of stability. In addition, Arizona, like much of the West, has a tense relationship with the federal government, which owns 70 percent of Arizona land. The state may exist only because of the federal investment, and yet the US government is viewed as an evil and distant interloper. Arizona's geography is insecure also because of an international border it cannot control.

A second factor is *institutional immaturity*. Arizona entered the Union as "The Baby State." This is not a nickname to create a sense of pride and high self-esteem. It was changed, fortunately, to the more macho "Grand Canyon State." Arizona is wedged in between two enormously populous and influential states, Texas and California, both of which have a strong self-identity. If the Texan caricature tends to be arrogant, the Californian image leans toward smug. Texas tell everyone not to mess with them, while California's attitude has been: "Hey, we're California, everyone knows we're the center of the universe."[6] Arizona, by contrast, was carved out of New Mexico—a state that is now one-third its size in population. Arizona does not have a coast, does not have a port, and was never a big rail center; overall, the reason for its existence is not self-evident.

The state is also relatively young. At the turn of the twentieth century, Colorado had almost ten times as many people as did Arizona. Now the states are of relatively comparable population size. Arizona boomed late and as a result did not develop many of the institutions that exist in other parts of the United States. There is no suite of liberal arts colleges started by every conceivable Protestant denomination like those scattered all over Ohio. The institutional higher-education base is three big state universities, a robust community college system, and an unusual for-profit education sector.

As to philanthropy, people tend to give to Milwaukee or wherever they came from rather than to Phoenix. Arizona came of age in an era of globalism. Just as it was becoming a serious city, all the big local banks disappeared. Phoenix has fewer headquarters of Fortune 500 companies than any big city in America. It is often the last US outpost before an industry goes offshore, like chip assembly plants or call centers.

So Arizona has institutional immaturity in a place of geographic insecurity, and on top of that it has an *unstable population*. In high-growth periods, for every five people who move in, three move out. More recently, the statistic is closer to four in and four out, making Arizona a desert encampment of nomadic people. In addition, the state lacks any dominant cultural influence. Utah has the powerful presence of the Mormon Church. There the church creates a backdrop, a set of relationships and shared expectations among citizens. New Mexico, similarly, has a dominant force in its Hispanic heritage, permeating the way that state thinks of itself. Though Arizona has major elements of both those influences, neither is dominant. In fact, the only dominant cultural group is transplants from the Midwest who moved because of mild winters and cheap houses.

The fourth factor that shapes Arizona is a history of *conservative populism*. The state was born in a spasm of early-twentieth-century populism. Initially, the politics were classically liberal and pro-labor. There remain remnants of that original populism: the entire legislature stands for election every two years. The state almost failed to be admitted to the Union because it wanted to be able to recall judges; William Howard Taft resisted statehood for so progressive an idea. But that populism began quickly to shift rightward. As Tom Frank wrote in *What's the Matter with Kansas?*: "The gravity of discontent pulls to the right."[7]

The pervasive Western myth is that of the rugged individual—the cowboy. The image of the West is a place where you can eke out a living in the desert with nothing other than a gun, a dog, a pickup truck, and maybe a chain-link fence. The reality is that you cannot do much of anything in a place like Arizona unless you get along well enough with your neighbors to share some kind of plumbing system. Historian Thomas Sheridan put it well: "Behind every rugged individualist stands a government agency."[8] Arizona is a place that exists by the dint of collective action. Yet Westerners distrust collective action because of this conservative populist bent. In large measure, the tax structure reflects this conservative populism. Arizona has among the highest business property taxes in the United States and among the lowest homeowner property taxes. What message does that send to the market? Answer: We want retired people to move here and buy houses, but we do not really care about companies.

Phoenix, like most of the new suburban cities, is a place where the social contract is still being negotiated. Because it is so immature institutionally, and because it is not sure what the sense of shared enterprise is, the nature of the social contract is unclear. Cities of nomadic transplants who live with walled backyards tend to think as individuals. If they do not like the "direction" their neighborhood is headed, they can leave. Perhaps they fail to join bowling leagues, tending to "bowl alone."[9] In most suburban cities, the trappings of urban political life in industrial cities—political machines, labor unions, community organizers—seem part of a dim and distant history. "Collective action" sounds slightly socialistic and sinister to many suburban city dwellers.

In thinking about the resilience and adaptability of urban areas in facing the challenges of the future, modern suburban cities may find themselves at an ironic disadvantage. Because the suburbs grew so quickly and were planned so deliberately, the possibility of change and adaptation has often been seen as a threat. A single-family home is the largest investment most Americans make in their lifetimes. In doing so, such investors are understandably nervous about the how potential changes might affect their investment. Further, a homeowner feels most comfortable living among people who have made a similar investment to his, and to bolster this reassurance, legal systems such as the zoning regulations imposed by municipalities have been created to protect neighborhoods against dramatic change. In most suburban cities, those regulations have made a very finely graded set of distinctions: 10,000-square-foot lots are separated from 14,000-square-foot lots. One of the strongest criticisms offered by New Urbanists is that this extreme form of segregation, based on lot size as a proxy for house cost (and therefore social group), is a negative consequence of suburban development. What it means for resilience and adaptability is that as houses on 14,000-square-foot lots become less economically viable, and as higher densities are needed to support alternative transportation systems or changing family patterns, such neighborhoods must be rezoned.

Rezoning in Phoenix can be a blood sport. Hearings are televised and often attract a surprising number of viewers. An area may be rezoned by the decision of a city council sitting in a legislative capacity, effectively changing the law as it relates to a given subdivision. Every zoning ordinance in Arizona contains a provision mandated by state law and drawn from the original standard Zoning Enabling Act of the 1920s, which mandates that a rezoning decision requires a supermajority (three-fourths) of the city council in the event that a certain number of neighbors protest. What this means is that shifting a large-lot neighborhood into zoning that would allow splitting lots or two homes per lot, or adding granny flats on the back of a lot, faces an extraordinary uphill battle against neighbors who fear any change in the status quo.

Changing the zoning in an existing suburban neighborhood is hard enough, but there is a bigger lurking problem with the future adaptability of suburban subdivisions. Starting in the 1950s, virtually every new subdivision had a set of "Covenants, Conditions, and Restrictions" (CC&Rs) that were imposed specifically to thwart change and adaptability. Originally, the CC&Rs were often used for the purposes of racial exclusion. The infamous exclusionary CC&Rs were voided by the US Supreme Court in 1948 in *Shelley v. Kraemer*.[10] But covenants continue to be used to impose a minimum size on houses in an area, to limit how many pets or animals can be kept, to create an architectural committee to review proposed houses to ensure that they are "harmonious and compatible," and to prohibit unsightly things like basketball backboards. Covenants have often come under fire for their restrictions on free speech in terms of flying the American flag or posting political signs at residences, which have been generally found to be protected by the First Amendment and therefore actions that cannot be prohibited by covenant. For-sale signs are often restricted in order to give the impression that no one in the neighborhood is trying to sell. Covenants have been used for all sorts of purposes. The legendary savings and loan executive Charlie Keating tried to impose covenants on a master-planned community in Phoenix to prohibit anyone in that community from keeping pornography in his house.

Unfortunately, the very thing that makes single-family houses so adaptable—the backyard space, garages, and carports where additions can be built or that can be converted to other uses—is very often prohibited by restrictive CC&Rs. Increasing the density in a neighborhood by adding a granny flat to the back of a lot, converting a garage to a bedroom, or building a second-story addition onto the back of a one-story home is often violative of the CC&Rs. There are hundreds of thousands of American homes built in areas where restrictive covenants give little flexibility to change or adapt to meet future conditions. Modifying or amending these restrictions is even more difficult than changing the zoning in a subdivision. Wholesale modification or amendment of covenants usually takes something on the order of three-quarters of the owners of a subdivision to agree—a nearly unattainable standard. Because these covenants are private contracts, it would be highly unusual for legislation at the state or federal level to interfere with an owner's contractual property rights. But the inability to modify covenants may actually ultimately work to cause the decline of some suburban neighborhoods rather than to enshrine the ideal suburban existence in perpetuity. At some point, it may be necessary to view some aspects of restrictive covenants as contrary to public policy in the same way the racial exclusions of the 1940s and 1950s came to be viewed.

The tip of the spear of the restrictive covenant issue may be the question of what to do with the excess number of golf courses built in places like Phoenix over the last several decades. There was a period of time where every major master-planned community seemed to center on a golf course. It was the amenity you needed in order to lure people to move to the Southwest with their sunny dream of retirement. Outside of Phoenix, the original Sun City includes no fewer than eight golf courses. The entire Phoenix metropolitan area has more than 200 courses. Some of these courses are municipal and some are associated with resort hotels, but most of those created within the last fifty years have been built as amenities for development. Many of the courses themselves never actually made enough money to fully pay for their ongoing maintenance costs (including water), much less for the underlying land value. But these courses made sense because the value of the lots surrounding the courses was increased so significantly that it made up for the decrease in the land value of the property actually occupied by the course.

Today there is a huge, well-documented decline in the number of golfers or the interest of baby boomers in seeking golf as their number-one goal in retirement. The Phoenix area alone may have twice as many courses as can economically survive.

To the extent that people paid premiums to look at and live on these golf courses, their interests were likely protected by an explicit covenant or deed restriction requiring that the course remain a golf course either in perpetuity or at least for a very long time. Even if there were not an explicit restriction, Arizona and a number of other Western states recognize an "implied restrictive covenant" doctrine, which holds that if a golf course was used as a marketing amenity and people paid a premium in the expectation it would be there, a restriction will be implied.[11]

With the decline in demand for golf, a number of these courses, including some that are explicitly restricted to remain golf courses, have today been shuttered and essentially abandoned. Standards that would demand unanimity, or three-quarters, or even a bare majority of homeowners under the restrictive covenant to approve the conversion of the golf course are almost surely impossible to meet.

Because of this quandary, courts will begin to fashion remedies allowing the modification or removal of deed restrictions. The acreage under these courses will then likely be redeveloped in a combination of higher-density housing and an alternative form of open space.

Sun City, Del Webb's prototypical retirement community on the west side of Phoenix, faces a CC&R problem beyond just golf courses. The community is both zoned and deed-restricted to limit the age of its full-time residents to fifty and older. These age-restrictive covenants are permitted because discriminating *in favor* of senior citizens is not illegal in the way that discriminating *against* them would be, and discriminating against younger people does not trigger strict scrutiny. Mounting evidence suggests that the baby boom generation is not as interested in purely homogenous communities of seniors the way earlier retirees were. This may result in such communities becoming less desirable and in property values being less stable. For these communities to change and adapt to have a fuller range of residents would require modifying both the zoning and the deed restrictions.

Other creative legal mechanisms that have flourished in newer cities can also result in impairing the ability of such cities to change and adapt. There are locations in the Phoenix metropolitan area today where suburban-style apartment complexes have been converted to condominiums, or where townhome communities were built adjacent to freeways, in which a transition to much higher-density residential or office uses would be supported by the market. These sites would be ripe for redevelopment. Because ownership is fractured into more than a hundred or more individual units by the condominium regime imposed on the property, reassembly of the site for redevelopment is a daunting, nearly impossible task. A single holdout can thwart the possibility of redevelopment entirely. Once upon a time, this sort of problem was handled by declaring a redevelopment area to be a "slum and blight" condition. A developer seeking to redevelop the property would then go out and acquire as many sites as possible, knowing that if there were a few holdouts the city could use its power of eminent domain to force a sale at fair market value for the purposes of completing the assembly. The use of municipal eminent domain for purposes of redevelopment has been all but completely halted in Arizona by Proposition 207 and a case called *Bailey Brake Shop v. City of Mesa*.[12] The proposition came into existence in the wake of the *Kelo* decision by the US Supreme Court, which authorized the use of eminent domain not just for redevelopment purposes but for economic-development purposes where the area being condemned was not necessarily in a "slum or blight" condition.[13] The outcry over this result was so intense as to cause an extreme backlash against the use of eminent domain by cities for anything other than straightforward construction of roads, parks, or other public amenities.

These particular challenges to making suburban cities resilient are driven by the strong but sometimes contradictory commitments in the United States to democratic decision making and also to the protection of individual property rights. These principles are sacred to Americans, particularly western Americans, and not likely to be compromised. The dilemmas they create, however, are very real.

Sustainability sometimes remains an elusive "I know it when I see it" concept. The myriad efforts to classify and rate the sustainability of cities may be useful in many ways, but they do not really address the question of whether a particular city is likely to survive. Some of these efforts fail to achieve this goal because they look only at the static measurements of how a city is performing as measured by a narrow metric at a particular point in time, which misses the entire matter of adaptation, change, and resilience. Some reviews base sustainability metrics on the "norms" of cities in wet or temperate climates very different from that of the desert Southwest. Some analyze only how seriously a municipal government takes its role in setting policy that is perceived as furthering sustainability.

The ultimate question of sustainability is how a particular place deals with its particular challenges over time. The challenges facing the Western cities of the arid Sunbelt are distinct from those facing wetter, cooler places. If there is one lesson to be learned from Phoenix about resilience and adaptability, it is how to accommodate a large city in a place with very little rain and no bodies of standing water. Political decisions made throughout the twentieth century created for Phoenix a robust and resilient watering system. The fact that the city has been able to bank trillions of gallons of water against future drought is evidence of that continuing commitment to resilience.

Throughout its life, Phoenix has had to cope with a difficult and challenging geography. Even in an era of increasing climate challenge, this past ability to deal with a severe climate suggests a future capacity to continue to do so. This is particularly true when the past challenge—a hot and dry climate—remains similar in kind to what will be faced in the future.

In a place that has long dealt with extremes and a high degree of uncertainty, an increase in the range and extent of that uncertainty can be met with the same kind of creative management that has worked before. In this, metro Phoenix may actually be better positioned to deal with the future than other places that relied on natural bounty and a temperate climate—and where climate change may portend dramatic changes.

The potential ubiquity of the impact of climate change on Phoenix runs the "frog in the boiling pot" risk—turn up the heat slowly, and the frog simply boils without ever thinking of escape. The threat to Phoenix's sustainability is the expectation that abundant land and sunshine, along with portable water and cheap housing and petroleum, will forever provide a winning formula. As climate challenges make a place built on climate less attractive, and as lifestyle and work patterns move beyond the age of the automobile, it would be easy for a place like Phoenix to miss out.

Suburban cities are not dying. They are becoming more dense, more diverse, more interesting, and more *urban*. And urban areas are, as the *Economist* found, becoming more livable, friendlier, softer, less dense, and more *suburban*. The confluence of urban and suburban forms is yet another demonstration of the thesis that cities are the products of millions of individual choices made in the context of a particular geography, technology, and government structure. There, of course, lies the central challenge of all sustainability: individual choices can add up to a collectively unsustainable condition. The challenge of sustaining any city is, quite simply, a manifestation of the tragedy of the commons. Managing that "tragedy" is the job of collective decision making. The story of Phoenix is a tale of adaptation and the power of collective action—government action—to confront the challenges of geography and respond through public policy. Canals and dams were constructed, highways and airports created connections, and a city was built in an unlikely place.

The future of all cities depends on a continuing capacity to navigate the social contract—to balance the dream of individual freedom with the challenge of a collective threat. For a city like Phoenix, the challenge may be greater—not because of climate, or density, or energy, but because, when you're sitting next to a private swimming pool, or driving alone in an air-conditioned car, it is too easy to forget about the historic social investments that made individual existence so comfortable. Suburban cities are designed around convenience, and the risk is that convenience begets complacency. The irony of sustainability is that greater challenges are more likely to precipitate more-robust solutions, so let us hope for an inconvenient future.

Afterword

Planning to Stay

I BELONG TO A BOOK CLUB OF ALL GUYS—LAWYERS, academics, businesspeople, washed-up politicians. We meet in a wine cellar at a resort that used to be owned by one of our members, and we indulge our egos and argue about politics, the economy, and the vicissitudes of life in Arizona. Sometimes we even talk about the book that we were supposed to have read.

Because we like cities, we have occasionally gone on study trips to other places and met with people who have written about or even helped to shape the cities we visit. In Chicago and Detroit, we looked at the decline and resurgence of the Midwest. In 2013, we went to New Orleans. I'd never been there before—a shameful omission on my part of any serious effort to study American cities. We "read" a slew of different books about the history and challenges of what Lawrence Powell termed "The Accidental City." One of these books was Tom Piazza's *Why New Orleans Matters*.

We went to the Lower Ninth Ward. We met with people who lived through Hurricane Katrina and were dealing with the serious challenges of sustaining a city in a very challenging place. We ate a lot, and I drank a Sazerac, which was genuinely awful.

The overwhelming message of the people we met and the things we read was one of passion. People love New Orleans with a fervent commitment that overwhelms myriad problems. They refused to abandon it after a catastrophic disaster because they could no more do so than abandon a family member who had fallen sick. New Orleans is not a sustainable city as measured by most sustainability metrics or specific wise policies. Measured on nearly any logical scale, it is not a sustainable place at all. But New Orleans survives because people care about it, believe that it matters, and will sustain it.

Does Phoenix matter? It is hard to find the same passion in a postwar suburban city. Commitment seems thin in a place so new and shiny, where few people have deep roots and an "old" building dates to 1960. As James Howard Kunstler put it in one of his diatribes against the suburbs: "What American boy will fight and die for a Taco Bell?" But Phoenix does matter. So do Las Vegas, and Orlando, and San Bernardino. These cities matter because millions of people live there and have invested in homes, businesses, churches, schools, roads, and parks, and because they like the way they live. These cities matter because they represent the urban pattern of a time—an urban pattern that has spread across the globe. Cities are built by millions of individual choices in the context of technology, economy, and politics.

Are these suburban cities sustainable? It's the same question as whether they matter. Sustainability isn't simply about per capita energy consumption, or locally grown food, or how far away water comes from. A city isn't sustainable because it hits a series of metrics that suddenly put it "in the zone." Cities don't exist in the binary options of "sustainable" or "unsustainable."

Cities are all about choices, trends, trajectories, and evolution. A city is resilient, is likely to survive, is working to sustain itself, because people want to live there—because they care about the future.

I can't answer for the rest of my book club, but I'm planning to stay.

Notes

Chapter 1

1. Richard C. Longworth, *Caught in the Middle: America's Heartland in the Age of Globalism* (New York: Bloomsbury USA, 2009).
2. Andrew Ross, *Bird on Fire: Lessons from the World's Least Sustainable City* (Oxford, UK: Oxford University Press, 2011).
3. William deBuys, "Phoenix's Too Hot Future," *Los Angeles Times*, March 14, 2013.
4. Zack Canepari, "Essay: A Planet of Suburbs, #3 Phoenix," *Economist*, December 6, 2014.
5. Jane Jacobs, *The Death and Life of Great American Cities* (New York: Random House, 1961).
6. The "concentration and dispersal" narrative draws heavily on Grady Gammage Jr., *Phoenix in Perspective* (Phoenix, AZ: Herberger Center for Design Excellence, Arizona State University, 1999).
7. Wallace Stegner, *Beyond the Hundredth Meridian: John Wesley Powell and the Second Opening of the West* (New York: Penguin Books, 1992).
8. "A Suburban World," *Economist*, December 6, 2014, 20.
9. Kenneth T. Jackson, *Crabgrass Frontier* (Oxford, UK: Oxford University Press, 1985).
10. Leigh Gallagher, *The End of the Suburbs: Where the American Dream Is Moving* (London: Portfolio, 2013). Continuing suburban trends are chronicled in many sources. See, e.g.: Emily Badger, "New Census Data: Americans Are Returning to the Far-Flung Suburbs," *Work Blog*, *Washington Post*, August 31, 2015.
11. James Howard Kunstler, *Home from Nowhere: Remaking Our Everyday World for the 21st Century* (New York: Touchstone Press, 1998).
12. See, e.g.: Robert Bruegmann, *Sprawl: A Compact History* (Chicago: University of Chicago Press, 2005); see also: Joel Kotkin, *The New Geography* (New York: Random House, 2000) and especially Kotkin's website, Newgeography.com.

13. William Whyte, *The Exploding Metropolis* (Chicago: University of Chicago Press, 1993).

14. Simon Winchester, *A Crack in the Edge of the World: America and the Great California Earthquake of 1906* (New York: Harper Perennial, 2006).

15. The World Commission on Environment and Development, *Our Common Future* ("Brundtland Report") (Oxford, UK: Oxford University Press, 1987).

16. Simon Bell and Stephen Morse, *Measuring Sustainability: Learning from Doing* (London: Routledge, 2003).

17. Richard Lawson, "The Worst 50 States in America: The Final Five," posted August 26, 2011, http://gawker.com/5834800/the-worst-50-states-in-america-the-final-five.

18. Sustainlane.com city rankings 2008. The sustainlane.com rankings appear to have disappeared after 2008. Their rankings appeared from 2005 to 2008.

19. See: "Green City Index," Siemens, October 2015, http://www.siemens.com/entry/cc/en/greencityindex.htm.

20. Reid Ewing, Rolf Pendall, and Don Chen, "Measuring Sprawl and Its Impact," Smart Growth America, www.smartgrowthamerica.org, 2002.

21. Tetratech, "Climate Change, Water, and Risk: Current Water Demands Are Not Sustainable," National Resources Defense Council (NRDC), http://www.nrdc.org/globalWarming/watersustainability/files/WaterRisk.pdf, July 2010.

22. Kate Brown and Cynthia Parpa, "Resilient Cities Research Report," *Grosvenor*, April 8, 2014, http://www.grosvenor.com/news-views-research/research/2014/resilient%20cities%20research%20report/.

23. Kent E. Portney, *Taking Sustainable Cities Seriously: Economic Development, the Environment, and Quality of Life in American Cities* (Boston, MA: MIT Press, 2013), 20.

24. Andrew Needham, *Power Lines: Phoenix and the Making of the Modern Southwest* (Princeton, NJ: Princeton University Press, October 2014).

25. Portney, *Taking Sustainable Cities Seriously*, 19.

26. Portney, *Taking Sustainable Cities Seriously*, 19, citing William E. Rees, "Is 'Sustainable City' an Oxymoron?," *Local Environment*, 2:3 (London: Routledge, 1997), 303–10.

27. Ronald Hansen, *Arizona Republic*, "Metro Phoenix May Be Missing the Bus," November 10, 2013. The listed cities are Atlanta, Austin,

Denver, Las Vegas, Philadelphia, Phoenix, Portland, Salt Lake City, San Diego, and Seattle.

28. See Portney, *Taking Sustainable Cities Seriously*, chapter 2, 36–87.

29. Randy Rodgers, "Will Vegas Be the First 'Net-Zero' City in America?," Sustainable City Network.com, April 3, 2013.

30. Ross, *Bird on Fire*, 15.

31. Ibid.

Chapter 2

1. Portions of this chapter have previously appeared in different forms in *Phoenix in Perspective*, in "Watering the Sun Corridor," and in Jack August and Grady Gammage Jr., "Shaped by Water: An Arizona Historical Perspective," in Bonnie G. Colby and Katharine L. Jacobs, eds., *Arizona Water Policy* (Tucson, AZ: Resources for the Future, 2007).

2. Sustainlane.com city rankings 2008. The sustainlane.com rankings appeared from 2005 to 2008.

3. Morrison Institute for Public Policy, Arizona State University, *Watering the Sun Corridor: Managing Choices in Arizona's Megapolitan Area*, August 2011. The City of Phoenix received ~186,000 acre-feet (AF) of Central Arizona Project water annually. (See: City of Phoenix Water Resources Plan [2011], https://www.phoenix.gov/waterservicessite/Documents/wsd2011wrp.pdf, 15–16.) On average, 50 percent of Phoenix's water supply comes from the Salt-Verde System, 44 percent from CAP supplies, 3 percent from groundwater, and 3 percent from treated effluent (see: City of Phoenix Water Resources Plan [2011], 12). Annually, the Phoenix Active Management Area (AMA) uses about 2.3 mega-acre-feet (MAF), 1.6 MAF surface water, and 700,000 AF groundwater. See: http://www.azwater.gov/AzDWR/WaterManagement/AMAs/Phoenix AMA/PhxAMAWaterManagement.htm.

4. Earl Zarbin, *Two Sides of the River: Salt River Valley Canals, 1867–1902* (Phoenix, AZ: Salt River Project, 1997), 86–87.

5. See: Wallace Stegner, *Beyond the Hundredth Meridian: John Wesley Powell and the Second Opening of the West* (New York: Penguin, 1992), 229.

6. Zarbin, *Two Sides of the River*, 124, 143, 193.

7. Ibid., 109–17, 177–91.

8. Bradford Luckingham, *Phoenix: The History of a Southwestern Metropolis* (Tucson, AZ: University of Arizona Press, 1995), 47.

9. Ibid., 164.

10. The upper basin includes Colorado, Wyoming, New Mexico, Utah, and the portion of Arizona above Lee's Ferry. The lower basin consists of the rest of Arizona, Nevada, and California.

11. Thomas E. Sheridan, *Arizona: A History* (Tucson, AZ: University of Arizona Press, 1995), 222–27.

12. On the CAP generally, see: Rich Johnson, *The Central Arizona Project, 1918–1968* (Tucson, AZ: University of Arizona Press, 1977).

13. Doug Kupel, *Fuel for Growth: Water and Arizona's Urban Environment* (Tucson, AZ: University of Arizona Press, 2003), 175.

14. Eric Holthaus, "Dry Heat," *Slate*, May 8, 2015, http://www.slate.com/articles/health_and_science/science/2015/05/arizona_water_shortages_loom_the_state_prepares_for_rationing_as_lake_mead.html.

15. Testimony of Arizona Department of Water Resources Director Tom Buschatzke, US Senate Committee on Energy and Natural Resources, June 2, 2015, http://www.energy.senate.gov/public/index.cfm/files/serve?File_id=6fcd8b5d-b4cd-4956-b0e1-574bfc65ebb5; see also: Yuma Efficiency Study, HDR.

16. Morrison Institute, *Watering the Sun Corridor*, 33–34.

17. The surface water–groundwater distinction was "discovered" by ProPublica in July 2015 (Anna North, "California's Big Groundwater Problem," *New York Times*, July 22, 2015) as an example of apparent mismanagement by Arizona and California, purportedly the two states forcing the worst water crises. The article did recognize Arizona's pioneering Groundwater Management Act, but made no mention of the groundwater replenishment the state has done.

18. See, e.g.: C. A. Woodhouse, D. M. Meko, S. T. Gray, and J. J. Lukas, "Updated Stream Flow Reconstructions for the Upper Colorado River Basin," *Water Resources Research* (Tucson, AZ: University of Arizona, 2006); University of Arizona, "Historic Colorado River Stream Flows Reconstructed Back to 1490," *Science Daily*, May 29, 2006.

19. USBR Lower Colorado Region Basin Studies, US Department of the Interior, Bureau of Reclamation, 2012, http://www.usbr.gov/lc/socal/basinstudies/, accessed November 3, 2015.

20. Ordinance No. 4634, City of Chandler, http://www.chandleraz.gov/content/20150528_6.PDF, accessed June 1, 2015.

21. Patricia Gober, *Metropolitan Phoenix: Place Making and Community Building in the Desert* (Philadelphia: University of Pennsylvania Press, 2005).

22. See, e.g.: American Housing Survey, 2011, US Census Bureau, https://www.census.gov/content/dam/Census/programs-surveys/ahs/publications/ahs11-21.pdf, accessed October 28, 2015.

23. See: City of Mesa, Arizona, High Water Use Action Plan, http://mesaaz.gov/home/showdocument?id=7460, accessed October 28, 2015.

24. Ibid.

25. Caitlin McGlade, "Why Our Water-Saving Ways in Metro Phoenix May Not Result in Lower Bills," *Arizona Republic*, October 30, 2015, 1; the article cites a recent study by Montgomery and Associates.

26. Tucson hydrologist and water policy expert Gary C. Woodard cites personal surveys in the Tucson area for the artificial turf–canine link.

27. See: "Tempe Town Lake Dam Bursts, Flooding River Bed," CBS News, July 21, 2010, http://www.cbsnews.com/stories/2010/07/21/national/main6698274.html.

28. Professor Nan Ellin, now at the University of Utah, while at Arizona State University led an effort called "Canalscape" to try to transform the canals of Phoenix, which, as she pointed out, has more miles of canals than does Venice.

29. See: "Water and Wastewater Service Pricing in Arizona: 2013–2014 Rates Survey Results," University of North Carolina Environmental Finance Center, 2014.

Chapter 3

1. Liz Osborn, "Hottest Cities in the United States," CurrentResults.com, http://www.currentresults.com/Weather-Extremes/US/hottest-cities.php, accessed October 28, 2015.

2. Liz Osborn, "Hottest Cities in the World," CurrentResults.com, http://www.currentresults.com/Weather-Extremes/hottest-cities-in-the-world.php, October 28, 2015.

3. Jerry Adler, "The Reality of a Hotter World Is Already Here," *Smithsonian Magazine*, May 2014, .

4. Much of the history of air-conditioning appeared in *Phoenix in Perspective*. Parts of this chapter also appeared in an earlier Morrison Institute paper, "Sustaining Phoenix," 2012.

5. Historical portions of this chapter are drawn from *Phoenix in Perspective*.

6. The credit to Carrier has been widely disputed. In Gail Cooper's book *Air-Conditioning America: Engineers and the Controlled Environment, 1900–1998* (Baltimore, MD: Johns Hopkins University

Press, 1998) gives the fullest account. In any event, Carrier is the best known and most popular early tinkerer with air-conditioning technology.

7. Malcolm Jones Jr., "Air-Conditioning," *Newsweek, Extra Edition 2000: New Millennium, the Power of Invention* (1997–1998), 42–43.

8. Cooper, *Air-Conditioning America*, 138.

9. Daniel E. Noble, "Motorola Expands in Phoenix," *Arizona Business and Economic Review* 3 (June 1954): 1–2.

10. Residential Energy Consumption Survey, US Energy Information Administration, 2009, https://eponline.com/articles/2011/08/22/air-conditioners-in-87-percent-of-u.s.-homes-though-not-all-meet-energy-efficiency-standards.aspx, accessed October 28, 2015.

11. Kate Murphy, "Enduring Summer's Deep Freeze," *New York Times*, July 4, 2015.

12. Daniel Engber, "Don't Sweat It," Slate.com, August 1, 2012, http://www.slate.com/articles/health_and_science/science/2012/08/air_conditioning_haters_it_s_not_as_bad_for_the_environment_as_heating_.html.

13. Daniel Engber, "Hot and Bothered," Slate.com, July 8, 2015, http://www.slate.com/articles/health_and_science/science/2015/07/air_conditioning_energy_ac_saves_lives_and_causes_less_climate_change_than.html.

14. Rory Carroll, "How America Became Addicted to Air-Conditioning," *Guardian*, October 26, 2015, http://www.theguardian.com/environment/2015/oct/26/how-america-became-addicted-to-air-conditioning, accessed October 28, 2015.

15. See: US Department of Energy, 2012 Strategic Sustainability Performance Plan, http://www1.eere.energy.gov/sustainability/pdfs/doe_sspp_2012.pdf, accessed October 28, 2015.

16. Michael Sivak, "Air-Conditioning versus Heating: Climate Control Is More Energy Demanding in Minneapolis than in Miami," *Environmental Research Letter*, March 27, 2013, http://iopscience.iop.org/article/10.1088/1748-9326/8/1/014050/meta;jsessionid=CEE9724DB89BDEDECD83DA5E1290606C.c1.

17. The Center for Climate Strategies, "Final Arizona Greenhouse Gas Inventory and Reference Case Projections 1990–2020," June 2005, http://www.climatestrategies.us/library/library/view/936.

18. Associated Press, "Solar Farm to Rise over 3 Square Miles in Arizona," NBCnews.com, March 7, 2008j, http://www.nbcnews.com/

id/23464740/ns/us_news-environment/t/solar-farm-rise-over-square-miles-ariz/#.VjwNHS1OmsY.

19. Solar Energy Industries Association, "2014 Top Solar States," http://www.seia.org/research-resources/2014-top-10-solar-states, accessed October 28, 2015.

20. Bill McKibben, "Power to the People," *New Yorker*, June 29, 2015, 34.

21. Ibid., 33.

22. The Salt River Project (SRP) provides both water and power to metropolitan Phoenix.

23. Darren Ruddell, Anthony Brazel, Winston Crow, and Ariane Middel, "The Urban Heat Island Effect and Sustainability Science: Causes, Impacts, and Solutions," *Sustainability for the 21st Century*, ed. David Pijanwka (Dubuque, IA: Kendall Hunt, 2015).

24. Tim Radford, "Air-Conditioning Raising Nighttime Temperatures in the US," *Guardian*, June 9, 2014.

25. Ray Quay et al., eds., *Greater Phoenix Regional Atlas: A Preview of the Region's 50-Year Future*, Morrison Institute for Public Policy, Center for Environmental Studies, Office of the Vice President for Research & Economic Affairs, Arizona State University (Phoenix, AZ: 2003), 62–65.

26. Peter Friederici, "Phoenix Tries to Rise from the Flames," *High Country News*, January 20, 2014.

27. Neil McMahon, "Can Melbourne Lower Its Average Temperature by 7 Degrees?," *Urbanland Magazine*, February 2, 2015.

28. See: Arizona Department of Environmental Quality, Air Quality Division, "EPA Clean Power Plan Stakeholder Process," https://www.azdeq.gov/environ/air/stakeholder.html, accessed October 28, 2015.

29. DeBuys, "Phoenix's Too Hot Future," *Los Angeles Times*, March 14, 2013.

30. The article cites a study published in the *Lancet* that looked at 74 million deaths in thirteen countries over nearly twenty years: 5.4 million were due to cold; 311,000 were due to heat.

Chapter 4

1. Phoenix's history with freeways is related in *Phoenix in Perspective*.

2. Bradford Luckingham, *Phoenix: The History of a Southwestern Metropolis* (Tucson, AZ: University of Arizona Press, 1995), 81.

3. Luckingham, *Phoenix*, 201.

4. Alex Shoumatoff, *Legends of the American Desert* (New York: Knopf, 1997).

5. For this history from a preeminent auto critic, see: Jane Holtz Kay, *Asphalt Nation* (Oakland, CA: University of California Press, 1997).

6. See, e.g.: Wikipedia, "General Motors Streetcar Conspiracy," https://en.wikipedia.org/wiki/General_Motors_streetcar_conspiracy, accessed October 28, 2015.

7. Robert Dunphy, "Passing Gridlock," *Urban Land*, November 1997.

8. Joel Nilsson, "Road to Oblivion: Papago Put Phoenix on the Path of Freeway Extinction," *Arizona Republic*, March 24, 1985.

9. Luckingham, *Phoenix*, 201.

10. Dunphy, "Passing Gridlock."

11. Patricia Gober, *Metropolitan Phoenix: Place Making and Community Building in the Desert* (Philadelphia: University of Pennsylvania Press, 2005), 153.

12. "MAP-Making Action Possible for Southern Arizona," *The Pothole Index 2013*, http://mapazdashboard.arizona.edu/article/pothole-index-2013, accessed October 28, 2015.

13. Texas A&M Transportation Institute, 2012 Urban Mobility Report, http://media2.kjrh.com/html/pdfs/2012urbanmobilityreport.pdf, accessed October 28, 2015.

14. Danile C. Vock, "How Car-Centric Cities Like Phoenix Learned to Love Light Rail," *Governing Magazine*, August 2015.

15. Brenna Goth, "Ahead of Prop 104, a Look at Who Uses Phoenix Transit," *Arizona Republic*, August 5, 2016.

16. See: http://www.governing.com/gov-data/car-ownership-numbers-of-vehicles-by-city-map.html, accessed October 28, 2015.

17. American Public Transportation Association, "Public Transportation Ridership Report," http://www.apta.com/resources/statistics/Documents/Ridership/2013-q4-ridership-APTA.pdf, accessed October 28, 2015.

18. 2010 American Community Survey, US Census Bureau, https://www.census.gov/programs-surveys/acs/, October 28, 2015.

19. American Public Transportation Association, "Public Transportation Ridership Report."

20. Urban Land Institute, "Myths and Facts about Transportation and Growth," Washington, DC, 1989.

21. Doug Short, "Vehicle-Miles Traveled: A Look at Our Evolving Behavior," *Advisor Perspective*, www.advisorperspective.com/dshort/update/DOT-Miles-Traveled, accessed August 20, 2015.

22. Eric Jay Toll, *Phoenix Business Journal*, March 24, 2015.

23. Matthew Cadell and Carlo Rotti, "Full Speed Ahead: How the Driverless Car Could Transform Cities," McKinsey & Company report, August 2015.

24. "What's Fueling Uber's Growth Engine," *Growth Hackers*, https://growthhackers.com/growth-studies/uber, accessed October 28, 2015.

Chapter 5

1. Michael Sorkin, "Can Williams and Tsien's Phoenix Art Museum Help This Sprawling Desert City Find Its Edge?," *Architectural Record* 1 (1997): 83–97; see also: Alex Shoumatoff, *Legends of the American Desert: Sojourns in the Greater Southwest* (New York: Knopf, 1997).

2. Jerry Adler, "Bye-Bye, Suburban Dream," *Newsweek*, May 14, 1995.

3. Robert Lang and Mark Muro, "Mountain Megas: America's Newest Metropolitan Places and a Federal Partnership to Help Them Prosper," Brookings Institution, July 20, 2008, http://www.brookings.edu/research/reports/2008/07/20-mountainmegas-sarzynski, accessed October 29, 2015.

4. The historical portions of this chapter are drawn from *Phoenix in Perspective*.

5. Bradford Luckingham, *Phoenix: The History of a Southwestern Metropolis* (Tucson, AZ: University of Arizona Press, 1995).

6. Quoted in: Witlold Rybozynski, *City Life* (New York: Touchstone, 1995), 109.

7. Grady Gammage Jr., *Phoenix in Perspective* (Phoenix, AZ: Herberger Center for Design Excellence, 1999), 251–54.

8. Greg Hise, *Magnetic Los Angeles: Planning the Twentieth-Century Metropolis* (Baltimore, MD: Johns Hopkins University Press, 1999).

9. *Infrastructure*, for these purposes, means sewer, water, and other utilities. The term is also generally inclusive of streets.

10. Clifford Edward Clark, *The American Family Home, 1800–1960* (Chapel Hill, NC: University of North Carolina Press, 1986).

11. Hise, *Magnetic Los Angeles*, 71–72.

12. Hise, *Magnetic Los Angeles*, 1–13.

13. Michael D. Jones, *Desert Wings: A History of Phoenix Sky Harbor International Airport* (Tempe, AZ: Jetblast Publications, 1997).

14. Bureau of the Census, *Statistical Abstract of the United States* (Washington, DC: US Printing Office, 1951), 522.

15. *Arizona Republic*, May 9 and December 8, 1955. See also: Luckingham, *Phoenix*, 161.

16. John A. Casazza and Frank H. Spink, *Shopping Center Development Handbook* (Washington, DC: Urban Land Institute, 1985).

17. *Arizona Republic*, March 24, 1928.

18. Rybczynski, *City Life*.

19. See: Casazza and Spink, *Shopping Center Development Handbook*; and Rybczynski, *City Life*, 206.

20. See, for example, 1957 aerial photos on display at the City of Phoenix Historic Preservation Office.

21. David Halberstam, *The Fifties* (New York: Ballentine Books, 1994), 134.

22. Ibid., 131.

23. Clifford Edward Clark, *The American Family Home* (Chapel Hill, NC: University of North Carolina Press, 1986).

24. Clark, *The American Family Home*.

25. Gary G. Peterson, "Home off the Range: The Origins and Evolution of Ranch-Style Architecture in the United States," *Design Methods and Theories* 23, no. 3 (1989): 1040–59.

26. Peterson, "Home off the Range," 1049.

27. Clark, *The American Family Home*.

28. "How to Start a One-Man Boom: The John Long Story," *House and Home*, February 1957, 117–18.

29. Clark, *The American Family Home*.

30. Ibid.

31. Rybozynski, *City Life*, 226–27.

32. Wendall Cox, "America's Desert Cities," *Huffington Post*, September 26, 2014.

33. Robert E. Lang, Andrea Sarzynski, and Mark Muro, "Mountain Megas: America's Newest Metropolitan Places and a Federal Partnership to Help Them Prosper," Brookings Institute, July 2008.

34. Luckingham, *Phoenix*, 193.

35. Anthony Downs, *New Visions for Metropolitan America* (Washington, DC: Brookings Institution Press, 1994).

36. Joel Garreau, *Edge City: Life on the New Frontier* (Harpswell, ME: Anchor, 1992).

37. In one controversial zoning case in 1981, the developers of the Phelps Dodge building at Central Avenue and Virginia Avenue actually hired international solar energy expert John Yellott to model the reflective

impact of the building on an adjoining neighborhood. The design of the building incorporated protruding vertical fins between the windowpanes. The fins were designed to shade the building's windows for the benefit of tenants but had the effect of breaking up the reflection of heat and light around the building as well and were dubbed "solar fins" as a result.

38. National Multifamily Housing Council, "Quick Facts: Resident Demographics," updated September 2015, http://nmhc.org/Content .aspx?id=4708, accessed October 29, 2015.

39. Joel Kotkin and Wendell Cox, "Where Are the Boomers Headed? Not Back to the City," NewGeography.com, October 17, 2003, http:// www.newgeography.com/content/003997-where-are-the-boomers-headed-not-back-to-the-city, accessed October 29, 2015.

40. The 1960 census listed 102,652,882 single-family homes in the United States. In 2013, the estimate was 197,327,583.

41. "Shifting Suburbia," Forum for Urban Design and the Museum of Modern Art, March 8, 2012, http://ffud.org/foreclosed/.

42. Joel Kotkin, "Don't Bet Against the (Single-Family) House," NewGeography.com, February 29, 2012.

Chapter 6

1. Richard Florida, "How the Crash Will Reshape America," *Atlantic Monthly*, March 2009.

2. John Collins Rudolf, "Construction That Fueled Growth in the Sun Belt Slows," *New York Times*, August 27, 2009.

3. Parts of this chapter are based on *Phoenix in Perspective*, and on the 2003 preface to the second edition, and on the Morrison Institute's reports "Megapolitan: Arizona's Sun Corridor," 2008; "Sun Corridor: A Competitive Mindset," 2014; and "The Future of Pinal," 2007.

4. Dennis Hoffman and Tom Rex, "The Economic Base of Arizona, Metropolitan Phoenix, Metropolitan Tucson, the Balance of the State, and Chandler," W. P. Carey School of Business, Arizona State University, June 2012.

5. Urban Land Institute, *Emerging Trends in Real Estate*, Washington, DC, 2013.

6. Chuck Bowden, *Trust Me: Charles Keating and the Missing Billions* (New York: Random House, 1993).

7. Jonathan Laing, "Phoenix Descending: Is Boomtown U.S.A. Going Bust?," *Barron's*, December 19, 1988.

8. Thomas E. Sheridan, *Arizona: A History* (Tucson, AZ: University of Arizona Press, 1995), 333.

9. Grady Gammage Jr., *Phoenix in Perspective*, 1st ed. (Phoenix, AZ: Herberger Center for Design Excellence, 1999), 58.

10. Grady Gammage Jr., *Phoenix in Perspective*, 2nd ed. (Phoenix, AZ: Herberger Center for Design Excellence, 2003), preface.

11. Ray Stern, "Tempe Rising," *Phoenix New Times*, June 19, 2014.

12. The new City Council voted in June of 2015 to cancel their existing deal with the Coyotes, citing a former city employee's conflict of interest. Then, two weeks later they approved a two-year extension with different terms.

13. Michael Orr, Arizona State University Real Estate Research Center, e-mail to author after reviewing his data, September 8, 2015.

14. Michael Lewis, *The Big Short: Inside the Doomsday Machine* (New York: W. W. Norton, 2010).

15. Rudolf, "Construction That Fueled Sunbelt Growth Slows."

16. Justin Hollander, *Sunburnt Cities* (London: Routledge, 2011).

17. Eric Jay Toll, "Why Velocity Will Fundamentally Transform the Phoenix Economy," *Phoenix Business Journal*, May 22, 2015.

18. Richard Florida, *The Rise of the Creative Class* (New York: Basic Books, 2012).

19. Robert Robb, "Phoenix Banks on the Peter Pan Theory of Millennials," *Arizona Republic*, August 12, 2015.

20. Enrico Moretti, *The New Geography of Jobs* (New York: Mariner Books, 2013).

21. Alia Beard Rau, "Arizona Tops Nation in College Cuts," *Arizona Republic*, May 13, 2015.

22. Michael Logan, *Desert Cities: The Environmental History of Phoenix and Tucson* (Pittsburgh, PA: University of Pittsburgh, 2006).

23. Arthur Nelson and Robert Lang, *Megapolitan America* (Chicago: APA Planners Press, 2011).

24. The Morrison Institute has issued two reports on the Sun Corridor: "Megapolitan: Arizona's Sun Corridor," May 2008; and "Sun Corridor: A Competitive Mindset," June 2014. This section draws heavily from these reports.

25. See: Gammage et al., "The Treasure of the Superstitions: Scenarios for the Future of the Superstition Vistas," Arizona State University Morrison Institute, April 2006.

26. Arizona State University Morrison Institute, "The Future at Pinal," July 2007.

Chapter 7

1. Jared Diamond, *Collapse: How Societies Choose to Fail or Succeed*, revised ed. (New York: Penguin Books, 2011).
2. Elizabeth Tandy Shermer, *Sunbelt Capitalism: Phoenix and the Transformation of American Politics* (Philadelphia: University of Pennsylvania Press, 2013).
3. William Frey, *Diversity Explosion: How New Racial Demographics Are Remaking America* (Washington, DC: Brookings Institution Press, 2014). An interactive cultural gap calculator is available at http://www.brookings.edu/research/interactives/2015/diversity.
4. Center for the Future of Arizona, "The Arizona We Want," Gallup Poll, 2009, http://www.thearizonawewant.org/assets/pdf/The_Arizona_We_Want.pdf, accessed October 29, 2015.
5. Ken Silverstein, "Tea Party in the Sonora," *Harper's*, July 2010.
6. See, e.g.: James Flanigan, *Smile Southern California, You're the Center of the Universe* (Palo Alto, CA: Stanford General Books, 2009).
7. Thomas Frank, *What's the Matter with Kansas? How Conservatives Won the Heart of America* (New York: Holt, 2005).
8. Thomas E. Sheridan, *Arizona: A History* (Tucson, AZ: University of Arizona Press, 1995).
9. Robert D. Putnam, *Bowling Alone: The Collapse and Revival of American Community* (New York: Simon & Schuster, 2001).
10. *Shelly v. Kraemer*, 334 US 1 (1948).
11. See, e.g.: *Shalimar v. D.O.C. Enterprises*, 688 P2d 682 (Az. App, 1984).
12. *Bailey v. Myers*, 76 P3d 898 (Az. App, 2003).
13. *Kelo v. City of New London*, 545 US 469 (2005).

Index

Note: Page numbers followed by the letter "f" or "t" indicate figures or tables respectively.

Activity nodes in suburban cities, 122–23
Adler, Jerry, 56
Aesthetics and urban environment in future of suburban cities, 47–50
Affluence, and suburbanization, 5
Agricultural areas and uses
  cooling effect at night, 67
  drought, 32–33
  efficiency of, in Arizona, 34
  in future of the suburban city, 41–42
  Imperial Valley's historic pattern of, 28
  residential conversion, 34
  water use, 39
Ahwatukee Foothills area, Phoenix, 2f
Air conditioning, 57–61, 58f, 98–99
Air quality, 69–70, 72, 79
Air travel, 4–5, 98–99
A. J. Bayless market chain, 101
American Continental, 128
Andrus, Cecil, and CAP project, 29–30
Arizona
  agricultural efficiency in, 34
  budget cuts, 141
  cultural generation gap, 155
  drought preparation in California vs., 33–36
  education in, 139–41, 140f–141f
  geography of insecurity, 156
  Groundwater Management Act, 24
  growth boundary defeat, 129–30
  income per capita, 139
  Mexico as trade partner with, 148
  politics in, 153–58
  population instability, 157–58
  Proposition 207, 146
  solar energy, 63
  water projects, reliance on, 26
  water use, population, and economic growth, 35f
  See also names of specific cities and counties

Arizona Canal, 25
Arizona Cardinals football team, 133
Arizona Corporation Commission (ACC), 63–64
Arizona Coyotes hockey team, 133
Arizona Public Service (APS), 64
Arizona State University (ASU), 39, 82–83, 131
Arpaio, Joe, 148
Artificial turf, in residential landscapes, 47, 69
Auto manufacturing, 77
Automobiles, 4, 75–77, 87–88
Autonomous vehicles, 89, 90f, 91–92

Baby boom generation, 87, 116–17, 162–63
Basin states, water source for, 28
Bayless market chain, 101
Bell, Simon, 11
Big box stores, decline of, 122
Bike-share systems, 88
Boom, in early 2000, 130
Boom-and-bust cycles, 126, 135, 136f, 137
Boomtowns, 95–96, 99, 130
Brookings Institution, study of "mountain megas," 108
Building forms, in postwar American, 99–100
Business and retail decentralization, 102
Bus rapid-transit, 84–85
Bus systems, 81–82

California
  drought preparation in Arizona vs., 33–36
  groundwater pumping limitations, 30
  Menlo Park—Visalia comparison, 138–39
  See also Los Angeles
Canal system, prehistoric, 26
CAP (Central Arizona Project), 8f, 29–30, 30f, 42
Carbon emissions from residential energy use, 62t
Carrier, Willis, 57

185

Carroll, Rory, 60
Carrying capacity, from water-supply
    perspective, 36
Carter, Jimmy, 29
CC&Rs (Covenants, Conditions, and
    Restrictions), 159–63
Central Arizona Project (CAP), 8f, 29–30,
    30f, 42
Chandler, Arizona, 43, 118, 130
Cities
    evolution of, 3–4
    hottest, 56
    hub and spoke, 106
    of postwar America, 108–9
    social contract and future of, 166
    See also Suburban cities; Sunbelt cities
Civano master-planned community, 45f
Clean Power Plan, 71–72
Climate change
    global warming vs., as moniker, 55–56
    potential adaptations to, 165
    predictions for, 61–62
    risk of complacency, 166
    Sunbelt cities and challenges of, 19–20, 73
    technology and, 62–63
CMBS (collateralized mortgage-backed
    securities), 134
CNU (Congress for the New Urbanism),
    113–16
Cold weather, deadliness of, 72
Collateralized mortgage-backed securities
    (CMBS), 134
Colorado River, 27–28, 32–34, 40
Colorado River Compact, 29
Community builders, 104
Congestion, of Phoenix compared to other
    US cities, 80
Congress for the New Urbanism (CNU),
    113–16
Conservatism of suburban cities, 19–20
Conservative populism, in Arizona, 158
Consumer housing surveys, 103
Cox, Wendell, 116–17
Credit default swaps, 135
Crow, Michael, 131
Cultural influences, lacking in Arizona,
    157–58
Curitiba, Brazil, 84–85

Data centers, water consumption, 43
Death and Life of Great American Cities, The

(Jacobs), 3
Density. See Residential density
Department of Water Resources (DWR),
    30–31
Desert cities, 31–32, 35
Detroit, Michigan, 137
Developers, horizontal and vertical, 96–97
Development, as industry, 98
Development patterns
    business and retail decentralization, 102
    changes in, 117
    Imperial Valley and, 28
    in postwar America, 123
    public transit and, 85–86
    of suburban cities, 86
Diamond, Jared, 153
Dominy, Floyd, 29
Droughts, 32–37
Ducey, Doug, 90
DWR (Department of Water Resources),
    30–31

Ecological footprint of cities, 14
Economic development, 42–43
Economist magazine, on world cities, 3
Economy
    diverse, in Phoenix, 127, 131, 150–51
    downturn (2005 to 2008), 126
    growth in, 35f, 135
    of innovation, 138
    natural advantages for stability in Sun
        Corridor, 14, 151
    strategies for improvement, 143–44
Education
    in Arizona, 139–41, 140f–141f, 157
    teacher salaries in Phoenix vs. other cities,
        141–43, 142f
Eminent domain, uses for, 163–64
Energy consumption, 14, 61, 62t
Engber, Daniel, 60
Entitled lots, in Arizona, 146
Evaporative coolers, 57

Federal government
    Arizona's relationship with, 156–57
    home construction involvement, 98,
        102–4
    investment in urban West, 154
    role in Western water issues, 25–26
FHA (Federal Housing Administration), 98,
    102–4

Florida, Richard, 125–26, 136, 138
Ford, Henry, 77
Foreclosure filings, in Phoenix compared to Las Vegas, 136
Freeway systems, 77–80, 81f

General Motors, 77
Geography of insecurity, 156
Gila River Indian Community, CAP water and, 42
Gilbert, Arizona, 114
Glendale, Arizona, 114, 132–33, 134f
Global warming. *See* Climate change
Gober, Patricia, 44
Golf course quandaries, 161–62
Graham, John, 137–38
Great Depression, 97–98
Greater Phoenix Economic Council, 137–38
Great Recession, 135, 137, 139–41
Grosvenor Resilient Cities Research Report, 13
Groundwater regulation, 13–14, 24, 30–31, 30f, 33
Growth
    in 20th-century Phoenix, 95–96
    forces in shaping of, 106–7
    as industry, 128, 135
    locations for, 43–44
    in Sun Corridor, 144f
    water and, 25, 35f, 41
Growth boundary defeat, Arizona, 129–30
Gruen, Victor, 104

Haboobs, 70–71, 71f
Heat waves, 56, 72–73
Hohokam people, 24, 153
Hollander, Justin, 136, 137
Home construction
    developer-driven model for, 103
    federal involvement in, 98, 102–4
    mass-production, 105–6
    "NextGen" model homes, 118, 120f
    on speculation, 96
Home mortgage loans, 133–34
Home ownership, 97–100, 105
Housing
    bubble, 125
    building permits, 129, 136f
    indigenous construction rejected by white settlers, 56–57
    market for, in proximity to shopping and entertainment, 116

postwar demand and financing for, 98, 102–3
    ranch houses, 100–101, 103–4, 118, 119f
Hub and spoke cities, 106
Human life, ingredients necessary for, 23–24
Human-powered transit, 86–87
Hydraulic fracturing ("fracking"), 73

Imperial Valley, 28
Indigenous construction, rejection by white settlers, 56–57
Industrial Revolution, 4, 73, 77
Infrastructure capacity, in resilience ratings, 13
Inner Loop freeway system, proposed, 78–79
Innovation economy, 138–39
Institutional immaturity, 156–59
Irrigation systems, Hohokam people and, 24

Jacobs, Jane, 3–4, 9
Jobs added in 1990–2011 among big cities in US, 150t
Johnson, Lyndon, 29
Jones, Malcolm, Jr., 57

Keating, Charlie, 128, 160
Kotkin, Joel, 116–17
Kyl Center for Water Policy (Arizona State University), 39

Laing, Jonathan, 128
Landscaping, in future of the suburban city, 46–47
Las Vegas, Nevada
    baby boomer generation, 117
    density of, 106–7
    Great Recession and, 135–36, 137
    growth and water challenges, 29
    housing bubble, 125
    sprawl ranking, 12
    sustainability goals, 17
Lewis, Michael, 135
Lifestyle and quality of life, 4, 23–24, 44–46, 95–96, 143
Light rail, 81–83, 82f, 85, 86f
Logan, Michael, 144
Long, John F., 104
Los Angeles
    air quality, 69, 79
    density of, 107
    development as industry in, 98
    MetroRail, 21f

urban heat island effect, 68
zoning ordinances, 109

Maricopa County
    air quality, 69–70
    automobiles registered in, 76
    building permits issued, 129
    climate change and, 12
    construction in, 135
    freeway system, 79
    new home construction, 135
    Pima County compared to, 144
    quality of life, 143
    solar installations, residential, 63
Maryvale, Arizona, 104–5, 105f
Mass-production of homes, 105–6
Megapolitan areas, 108, 145, 147t, 149
Megapolitan thinking, benefits of, 148
Menlo Park, California, 138–39
Mesa, Arizona
    GRID Bike Share, 88
    light-rail line, 81
    population, 1, 130
    Proposition 207 and, 163
    public transit use and walking, 87
Mexico, as trade partner with Arizona,
    148
Misting systems, 69
Moeur, B. B., 23
Moretti, Enrico, 138–39
Morrison Institute, Arizona State University,
    35–36, 41
Morse, Stephen, 11
Multi-family projects, 48f, 116
Murphy, Kate, 59–60
Murphy, William J., 25
Museum of Modern Art, 117–18

Napolitano, Janet, 63
Natural advantages for economic stability in
    Sun Corridor, 14, 151
Natural environment in future of the
    suburban city, 50–51
Needham, Andrew, 14, 60
Neighborhoods, transitional, 123
Neighborhood sociability, demise of, 59
New Deal policies, 97–98
New Urbanism, 113–16, 115f
"NextGen" model homes, 118, 120f

Ozone, in Maricopa County, 70

Parker Dam construction, 23
Parking lots, 101
Pedestrian amenities in suburban cities, 114–16
Philanthropy, in Arizona, 157
Phoenix
    aerial view, 93
    Ahwatukee Foothills area, 2f
    annexation policies, 99–100, 106
    as boomtown, 98–99, 130
    city lights at dusk, 94f
    climate change and, 66–67, 165
    condominiums, 120, 121f
    downtown, 9f, 110–11
    economic diversity, 127, 131, 150–51
    foreclosure filings, 136
    growth in 20th century, 95–96
    high-rise buildings, 111–12
    income average per capita, 140f
    institutional immaturity, 158–59
    modern history, 94–95
    redevelopment potential, 163
    residential density, 106–7
    rezoning challenges, 159–60
    Rio Salado restoration area, 49
    stock market crash (1989) and, 129, 133
    street grid, 78, 80–82, 84–85
    as suburban city prototype, 112
    success of, 149–50
    transit-oriented development, 83
    transportation plan (2015), 83–84
    Tucson compared to, 143–45, 144f
    See also Sun Corridor (Phoenix—Tucson
        urban region)
Phoenix Planning Commission, 110–11
Pima County, Maricopa County compared
    to, 144
Politics in Arizona, 153–58
Population
    changes in, by megapolitan area, 147t
    economic growth, water use, and, 35f
    growth of, in Sun Corridor, 144f
    instability of, in Arizona, 157–58
    of Mesa, 1, 130
Portney, Kent, 14, 17
Postwar America, 99–104, 108–9, 123
Pothole Index rankings, 80
Powell, John Wesley, 25, 31
Precipitation, in Arizona vs. California, 33
President's Conference on Home Building and
    Home Ownership, 97–98
Problem of the last mile, 88–89

Property right to development, 146
Public transit, 84–86
    See also Light rail
Pulliam, Eugene, 78–79

Quay, Ray, 44

Rail system, proposed, 79
Ranch houses, 100–101, 103–4, 118, 119f
Ranch-house suburbs, and home ownership,
    105
Real estate development, 126
Reclamation era, 24–25
Reclamation Service, 26
Rees, William, 14
Residential density
    declines in, for world cities, 3
    in future of the suburban city, 44
    infill development, 114
    of major metropolitan regions, 107–8,
        107t
    of Phoenix, 106–7
    realistic view, 110f
    simplistic view, 109f
Resilience of suburban cities, 12–14, 153–54,
    159–60, 164
Retail, as changing aspect of urban
    development, 100–102, 116, 122
Ride-sharing companies, 90–92
Rio Salado restoration area, Phoenix, 49
Riparian or wetland habitat, ramifications of
    loss of, 50–51
Robb, Robert, 138
Roosevelt, Franklin D., 97–98
Roosevelt, Theodore, 27
Roosevelt Dam, 26–27, 27f
Ross, Andrew, 2, 17–18
RTC (Resolution Trust Corporation), 128–29

Salt River Project (SRP), 27, 40, 49f, 50, 65
Salt River Valley, 26–27, 94–95
Savings and loan deregulation, 127–28
Scenic Airways, 98–99
Scottsdale, Arizona, 49, 49f, 50, 85, 114–16,
    130
Self-driving cars, 89, 90f, 91–92
Settlement patterns of the American West, 6,
    25, 94–95, 112–13
Shopping centers, 100–102, 116, 122
Siemens Green City Index, sustainability
    ratings by, 12

Silverstein, Ken, 156
Single-family homes
    adaptability of, 118, 120
    building permits in boom and bust of
        metro Phoenix, 136f
    dominance of, as preferred lifestyle, 4
    mass-production of, 105–6
    multi-generational, 118, 120f
    as predominant choice of most Americans,
        117
Sky Harbor airport, 98–99
Skytrain, 83, 84f
Smart Growth America, sustainability
    rankings by, 12
Smart mobility, 88–89
Social contract, and future of cities, 166
Social equity, heat and poor air quality as
    threats, 72
Societal extinction, factors in, 153–54
Solar energy, 63–65, 64f
Sonoran Desert, 70–71
SRP (Salt River Project), 27, 40, 49f, 50, 65
Starter homes, 105–6
State Farm regional headquarters, on Tempe
    Town Lake, 150–51
State Trust land, Arizona, 145–46
St. Louis, Missouri, 1
Stock market crash (1989), 129
Streetcars, demise of, 76–77
Subdivisions, 45f, 96–97, 104, 118
Subprime mortgages, 134–35
Suburban bashing genre in American
    literature, 6
Suburban cities
    activity nodes in, 122–23
    conservative bent of, 154
    criticism of, 18–19
    defense of, 6
    development patterns of, 86, 105–6
    future of, 8–9
    hallmarks of, 7–8
    in last half of 20th century, 2–3
    negative consequences of, 159
    pedestrian amenities in, 114–16
    Phoenix as prototype for, 112
    resilience, 12–14, 153–54, 159–60, 164
    transportation and land-use changes in,
        20–21
    water rates, future, 51–52
Suburbanization forces, 5
Suburban sprawl, 6–7, 12, 19

Suburbs, origins of and reactions to
    term, 5–6
Sunbelt capitalism, 154
Sunbelt cities
    air conditioning and livability of, 19–20
    climate change, challenges of, 73
    sustainability challenges, 17
    sustainability rankings for, 11–13, 15
Sun City, CC&R problem, 162–63
Sun Corridor (Phoenix-Tucson urban region)
    Arizona Proposition 207 and, 146
    demographics, changing, 146–48
    density, compared, 109f
    as emerging megapolitan region, 108, 145
    Mexico, relationship with, 148–49
    natural advantages for economic stability in,
        151
    water supply, 33, 36, 38–41
    water use, 41–43, 45f, 46
Supermarkets, 101
Superstition Freeway (US Route 60), 81f
Superstition Vistas, 145
Surface parking, 101
Sustainability
    climate change and, 19–20
    components of, 10f
    economic, 151
    metrics of, 11, 16, 164–65
    origins and definition of, 10
    policy choices and, 16, 37–38
    rankings for, 12–13, 15, 17
    as rubric, 2
    of Sunbelt suburban cities, 11–12
    threats to, 165–66
    use of term, 9
Sustainlane.com, sustainability ratings by,
    12, 13
Swilling, Jack, 94–95
Swimming pools, private vs. shared, 44–46

Taxi service, ride-sharing companies
    compared to, 90–91
Tax revenues vs. education spending in
    Arizona, 141f
Tax structure, in Arizona, 158
Technology, in climate change mitigation,
    62–63, 72–73
Tempe, Arizona
    bike share program, 88
    high-density infill, 114
    light-rail line, 81–82, 85

refocus of, 131–32
    townhomes, 121f
    Town Lake, 5f, 47–49, 131–32, 132f,
        150–51
    Transportation Center, 16f
    walkability, 114
Tenements, Industrial Revolution and, 77
Townhomes, Tempe, 121f
Tragedy of the commons, 166
Transit
    bus rapid-transit, 84–85
    bus system, 81–82
    human-powered, 86–87
    light rail, 81–83, 82f, 85, 86f
    public, 85–87
Transit-oriented development, 83
Transportation
    and land-use changes in suburban cities,
        20–21
    plan for City of Phoenix (2015), 83–84
    problems in, and non-transportation
        solutions, 91
    transformations of, 87–88
    Uber, Lyft, and revolution in, 89–91
    of water, 24
Tucson, Arizona
    megapolitan thinking, benefits of, 148
    Phoenix compared to, 143–45, 144f
    Pothole Index ranking, 80
    relationship with Mexico, 148
    See also Sun Corridor (Phoenix-Tucson
        urban region)

Uber, 90
Udall, Stewart, 29
University of Arizona, 149
Urban and suburban forms, confluence of,
    165–66
Urban canyons, 67
Urban change agents, 4
Urban heat islands, 20, 46–47, 65–67, 67f,
    68–69
Urbanization in the American West, 4–5,
    93–94, 108
Urban resilience, 12–14, 153–54, 159–60, 164
Urban village concept, 111–12
Utility companies and solar power, 63–64

Valley Metro light-rail system, 81–83, 85
VA (Veterans Administration) mortgages,
    102–3

Vehicle-miles traveled, changes in, 87
Vehicles, alternative-fuel and electric, 87–88
Velocity effort, 137–39
Visalia, California, 138–39
Walkability, New Urbanism and, 113–16
Water
    as basis for planning Western growth and
        settlement, 25
    federal government's role in issues
        regarding, 25–26
    price of, among largest US cities, 52t
    rates in future suburban cities, 51–52
    reality of, in the desert, 5, 31–32, 35
    in resilience ratings, 13–14
Watering the Sun Corridor (Morrison
    Institute), 35–36
Water management
    banking in underground aquifers, 33–34
    against future assumptions, 37
    heat island effect and, 68
    for irrigation in central Arizona, 28f

reserves for future alternative developments, 43
    transportation of, 24
Water rights, Colorado River, 27–28,
    38–39
Water supply, as dilemma, 19, 40–41
Water usage
    in Central Arizona, 35f
    curtailed, in Arizona, 34
    by data centers, 43
    as focus of development, 49
    in metro areas of the US, 36–37, 37t
    in Phoenix, 36
    residential density and, 44
    in Sun Corridor, 38–39, 41–43, 45f, 46
Western myth, collective action vs., 158
Winchester, Simon, 9–10
Wood-burning fireplaces, 70
World cities, hottest, 56
World War II, 98–99, 123

Zoning ordinances, 96, 109, 159–60